THE POWER
OF
PLANETS

P. Khurrana

Rupa & Co

Typeset in 11 pts. Revival by
Nikita Overseas Pvt Ltd,
1410 Chiranjiv Tower,
43 Nehru Place
New Delhi 110 019

Printed in India by
Gopsons Papers Ltd.
A-14 Sector 60
Noida 201 301

THE POWER
OF
PLANETS

Dedicated to Her Holiness
my mother late Smt. Raj Khurrana

Those who know Astrology only Indicate
in a way what will take place in the future.
Who else, except the Creator Brahma,
can say with certainty what will definitely happen?

Contents

Acknowledgement

I express my gratitude to my Guru Swami S. Chandra ji, who selflessly set my bearings right, who baptised me by involving the Powers that be and ushered me into the depths of Hindu as well as Western astrology.

I thank Ramikka for her hard work, devotion and efficient managing of my work schedule and office.

To R.D. Khurrana, my father, I owe a lot who has given me blessings and good *sanskaras* in the true sense of the word. The help and support I received from my wife Poonam and my children Ayushmaan and Aparshakti who made it possible for me to lead a fairly normal life and to be a successful astrologer.

I thank my sister Chandra Kanta for her warm support and Sat Pal ji for his ideal relationship.

I thank my friends, brothers and their wives for their encouragement and continued patience for not disturbing me me during my hectic work schedule.

My heart goes out unquestioningly to thank Tomms Babrrani Bravocorr whose unconditional love and emotional support

x   The Power of Planets

eased my adjustments to a strange way of life' and who made
the writing of this book a joyous task.

And last yet not the least, I express my thanks to my
publishers and their team for their most valuable contribution
to make this work a complete success.

Office: **P. Khurrana**
Hotel Shivalikview, Sector 17
Chandigarh (India)
(0172)-703018, 712280, 563937
www.astroindia.com
email: pkhurrana@astroindia.com

Stars in Your Life

Their effect on human destiny has been charted for more than 5000 years, yet why do astrologers' works remain something of a mystery? Here we explain how the stars apply their influence on daily life.

It is known from the ancient horoscopes imprinted on clay tablets, which have been unearthed, that a type of astrology was practised almost 5300 years ago. However, no one knows for certain just how, when and where astrology first began, although we do know it flourished.

Astrology was practised in ancient Chaldea, Mesopotamia, Babylon and Egypt. Surely, anything which has persisted for so long must contain some element of eternal truth.

It is a worthless and meaningless exercise for people with no knowledge of scientific astrology to criticise the subject and dismiss it as rubbish; these people merely demonstrate their own ignorance. Throughout the world there are many excellent professional astrologers who are highly educated and intelligent. They practise astrology because they know it works – it is as simple as that.

Of course, why it works remains a mystery. Many theories have been propounded – electro-magnetic fields, radiation and so on – but I am inclined to agree with the ancient astrologers who believed in a divine unity between man and the universe. If this is true, we not only live within this solar system, we also are an inseparable part of it. Because of this invisible interrelationship, everything which happens in any part of the solar system has a corresponding effect on all other parts, including each individual. That may seem a sublime concept but, somehow, it 'feels' right. Coming down to Earth, let me tell you a little about a horoscope and how it works.

The main components which go into the making of a horoscope are the Sun, the Moon, the eight known planets – Mercury, Venus, Mars, Jupiter, Saturn, Uranus, Neptune and Pluto – plus the 12 signs of the Zodiac. Our own planet Earth also is used because it plays a vital role in determining some very important, sensitive points such as 'the ascendant', which corresponds with the eastern horizon, and 'the descendant' point on the western horizon.

If an astrologer knows the date, place and time of any event, he or she can calculate a horoscope from it. It could be the birth of an idea, the birth of a question which needs to be answered or the incorporation of a company, the birth of a baby, the opening of a new business, the start of a long journey, the birth of an animal, the starting time of a race, the launching of a ship, the birth of a nation or even the first 'on-sale' date of a magazine.

A horoscope is simply a map of the heavens showing the exact positions, at a given time, of the Sun, Moon and planets within the framework of the zodiac in relation to a particular place on Earth. The mathematical process of casting a horoscope involves the science of astronomy, while interpreting all the factors in the horoscope chart involves the art of astrology. I shall not explain the technical and mathematical process of calculating the actual horoscope, but provide an in-depth scope of a particular planet of Zodiac sign and respective house with suggestive remedies. There are twelve parts of the Zodiac sign called *Rashis*. Each sign of the Zodiac is 30 degrees in extent. The Zodiacal signs are tabulated as below:

Sign	Extent	Represented by	Number denoting the sign
Aries	0-30 degrees	Ram	1
Taurus	30-60 degrees	Bull	2
Gemini	60-90 degrees	Pair of lovers	3
Cancer	90-120 degrees	Crab	4
Leo	120-150 degrees	Lion	5
Virgo	150-180 degrees	Maiden	6
Libra	180-210 degrees	Balance	7
Scorpio	210-240 degrees	Scorpion	8
Sagittarius	240-270 degrees	Bow	9
Capricorn	270-300 degrees	Crocodile	10
Aquarius	300-330 degrees	Pot	11
Pisces	330-360 degrees	Pair of fish	12

Grouping of Signs

The signs can be categorised into three groups from Aries onwards. They are termed as moveable or cardinal, fixed and common or mutual. Moveable signs indicate an energetic and dynamic nature; fixed signs, a tenacious and stubborn nature; common signs, a changeable nature.

Moveable	Fixed	Common
Aries	Taurus	Gemini
Cancer	Leo	Virgo
Libra	Scorpio	Sagittarius
Capricorn	Aquarius	Pisces

Each sign starting from Aries onwards is also subsequently termed as odd (or male) and even (or female). All odd signs are cruel and masculine and all even signs are mild and feminine.

Odd	Even
Aries	Taurus
Gemini	Cancer
Leo	Virgo
Libra	Scorpio
Sagittarius	Capricorn
Aquarius	Pisces

The Signs can also divided into four groups, representing the basic elements – fire, earth, air and water. Thus the signs, starting from Aries onwards are termed subsequently as Fiery, Earthy, Airy and Watery.

Fiery	Earthy	Airy	Watery
Aries	Taurus	Gemini	Cancer
Leo	Virgo	Libra	Scorpio
Sagittarius	Capricorn	Aquarius	Pisces

Significance of the houses

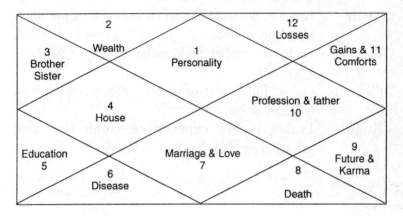

Significance of the houses: The twelve houses (as usually understood) in the horoscope signify different aspects of a man's life as given below:

House

First: Personality, body, face, appearance, health.
Second: Wealth, speech, family, neck, throat, right eye.
Third: Brother or sister, courage, short journeys, hands, right ear.
Fourth: Education, mother, house or land, convenience, general happiness, maternal uncle, chest.
Fifth: Children, intelligence, fame, position, love, stomach.
Sixth: Diseases, debts, sorrows, injuries, notoriety, aunt or uncle, waist, enemies.
Seventh: Marriage, desires, sexual diseases, loins.

Eighth: Death or longevity, sexual organs, obstacles, unearned wealth, accident.

Ninth: Fortune, character, religion, father, long journeys, grandson, thighs.

Tenth: Profession, father, rank, authority, honour, success, knees.

Eleventh: Gains, fulfillment of desires, prosperity, friends, left ear, ankle.

Twelfth: Losses, misery, expenditure, comfort of bed, salvation or moksha, feet, left eye.

The Twelve Sectors

Most people know there are 12 Signs of the Zodiac but not many are aware of the fact that there also are 12 others divisions of the horoscope – the 12 sectors. Most textbooks on astrology refer to these as the 12 Houses of the horoscope.

These 12 divisions of the heavens relate to the common, everyday affairs of people's lives, such as finance, home, marriage, career, travel and so on. They also relate to hundreds of other matters with which we fill our lives, but I shall not complicate the issue by going into such details. You can see a simplified version of the 12 sectors in the figure on p. 5.

The Sun, Moon and each of the planets produce their own unique effects. For example, Jupiter brings increase and expansion, whereas Saturn produces decrease and limitation. Therefore, it is easy to see that person A who was born with Jupiter in division number two i.e. the financial sector, will generally be much better off financially than person B with Saturn in that same sector. The date of birth determines in which Signs of the Zodiac, the Sun, Moon and all the planets will be placed but it is the hour and place of birth which determines which sectors (or houses) of the horoscope these bodies will occupy.

AFFAIR OF THE TWELVE SECTORS

First Sector

This always corresponds to your birth sign or Star sign. For example, if you are an Aquarian, Aquarius rules your First Sector. Therefore, it relates to your personal life, personality, interests, the way you think, feel and live, plus the manner in which you react to other people and situations. It represents you as a person and therefore, the image you project which other people see. It also represents your marriage partner, competitors, rivals, enemies and business associates. The First Sector relates to the beginning and to the start of anything new, such as a/an project, association, idea, interest, activity, trend or condition.

Second Sector

The Second Sector relates to your income, personal financial affairs, expenses, the way you earn and spend your money, profits and losses, your wage level, personal possessions and the things you buy for yourself or others. It also covers small items which other people buy for you, bank accounts, cheques, financial documents and your attitude to money matters. Because financial affairs play such a significant role in the way people live, it is obvious that the Second Sector is very important.

Third Sector

The Third Sector relates to all forms of communication – mental and physical – such as mail, correspondence, newspapers, magazines, writers, advertisements, agents, contacts, phone calls, public transport, your car, taxis, or other means of travel, short trips, outings, errands, deliveries, discussions, interviews, debates, conferences, gossip, chatter and rumours. It also relates to the type of mind you have, your mental interests, thinking habits and general attitude to people and circumstances. The Third Sector gives indications concerning matters which either involve or affect neighbours and close relatives. These matters especially concern your brothers and sisters.

Fourth Sector

The Fourth Sector rules your home, family circle, and all matters concerning the domestic front, including the building, block of land and everything in and around the house. This sector gives indications about visitors, house guests, lodgers, intruders, burglars and others who call at your place, whether invited or uninvited, welcome or unwelcome. It also rules any additional property or real estate interests you may have now or in the future.

Fifth Sector

The Fifth Sector relates to many of the things we think of as goodies, such as pleasure, parties, entertainment, amusement, holidays, relaxation, social life, artistic, creative, musical and cultural pursuits, luxuries, celebrations, banquets or dinner parties, movies, dancing. It also rules places where any of these activities are carried out. This sector relates to romance, courtship, love affairs, emotional experiences, your sweetheart or lover and your children. Commonly known as the sector of luck, it rules gambling and all forms of speculation such as lotteries, the pools, lotto, casinos, racing, the stock market and any other activity where the element of chance is involved.

Sixth Sector

The Sixth Sector rules a wide range of matters which come under the basic categories of work and health. Elaborating on these two fundamental themes, it can include such things as service rendered or received, duties performed for or under another person; to assist, hold or obey a superior; ordinary routine work and daily chores; employees, staff, servants, hired help, the workforce and the working classes, people who are in subordinate positions; the place where you work and the conditions under which your work is done, the various problems, obstacles, opportunities and success in connection with your job, your relationships with workmates and business colleagues, health, sickness, hygiene, dietetics.

Seventh Sector

The Seventh Sector relates to partnership, marriage, close personal or business relationships, marriage partner or the person with whom you live and share all things, co-operation, mutual interests and activities, broken partnerships such as separation or divorces and marital discord. The Seventh Sector also gives indications concerning emotional, business, financial or sporting rivals, opponents, competitors and open enemies.

Eighth Sector

The Eighth Sector has a connection with financial affairs which involve other people or their money, such as a loan from another person, bank, finance company, building, society or insurance company. It covers joint financial interests, your partner's income, shares, insurance claims, a legacy, inheritance, will, deceased estate matters, taxation, money owed to you or by you, investment profits or losses, financial condition after marriage and money from sources other than your regular income. The Eighth Sector also has a connection with such things as astrology, clairvoyance, mysticism, psychic awareness, occult science, chemistry and other methods of trying to unravel the mysteries of life, death and nature's secret forces.

Ninth Sector

The Ninth Sector is often called the area of the higher mind because it is connected with literature, law, philosophy, religion, scientific thought, higher education and anything else which broadens the mind, expands your awareness and widens your mental and physical horizons. It is related to distant people and places, foreign countries, long-distance travel, foreign customs and commodities, imports, exports, overseas contacts and correspondence.

Tenth Sector

The Tenth Sector rules your profession, career, status, ambitions, business, prestige, achievements, worldly goals and activities, public image, position and reputation, professional qualifications and business opportunities. It is the gateway to success from the lowest to the highest. Depending on what planetary influences are focusing on this sector at any given time, it can bring either failure, mild satisfaction, success, recognition, promotion, honour, fame or glory. The Tenth Sector is your own Mount Everest and how far your climb it is up to you. It also relates to people in positions of power and authority including your boss and other superiors.

Eleventh Sector

The Eleventh Sector relates to the personality and character of your friends as well as to your relationship with them. This is the link with your social acquaintances and it will indicate when periods of harmony, discord, fidelity or falsehood can arise with or through such people. This sector also relates to societies, fraternal groups, clubs, brotherhood, fellow feeling and any gathering of people for a common purpose. The Eleventh Sector gives indications about your hopes, wishes and aspirations.

Twelfth Sector

The Twelfth Sector is the most secret, veiled, mysterious area of your solar horoscope. It rules private or confidential matters, hidden places or things, activities which are carried on behind the scenes or in seclusion, places of confinement such as hospitals, institutions or prisons, people who are confined or handicapped, secrets, mysteries, puzzles, secluded areas, things in the background of your life, physical, mental, emotional or moral bondage, loneliness, being shut out or cut off, restriction, denial or self-denial, phobias, secret fears, hidden pitfalls, underhandedness, intrigues, locks, the unseen.

The Sun

The Sun symbolises the leader, the husband, the political chief, the father. It radiates heat and is positive. Its colour is orange and the element is a mixture of air as well as fire. Its domicile is in Leo, exile is in Virgo, exaltation is at 19 degrees of Aries and it falls in Libra. The planet is slightly arid but is still advantageous for financial issues and business venture. It gets and enlists the aid of people in power and position. It exercises authority over the metal gold and the seventh day of the week, that is, Sunday. In a draw of the cards, the Sun represents the day since it gets radiance, fortune, progress and steadiness in all concerns.

This planet exercises a distinctive effect on the heart and should be regarded as the Lord of Life (unless it is not very strong). It should be perused carefully with reference to health matters. Its position is significant, both from the perspective of its situation in the House and of the Sign in which it lives since it symbolises the ruler of nativity.

THE SUN IN THE HOUSES

The Sun in the First House

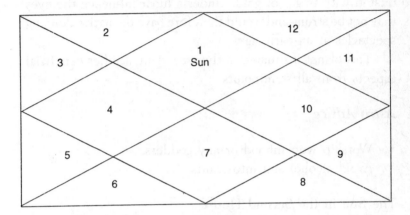

This situation of the Sun is a sign of a fortunate and long life (unless the Sun is weak) in keeping with the native's status in society. It fuels him with ambition and high goals and moulds him into a fair and kind-hearted soul.

The life of the native will be a point of admiration for everyone who meets him, as a result of which he will be the leader, the boss, someone to be reckoned with. More often than not, the native may unconsciously provoke jealousy and ill-will amongst the ones he defeats or obstructs and hence may have quite a few adversaries.

He is of a dignified carriage, average height and blessed with immense energy and enthusiasm. Though he may look fragile he has great strength and though his muscles may not be as well defined as in the case of Mars, they are highly flexible and resilient.

The native's entire being, physical and moral is diffused and infused with equilibrium and accord. Complexion is smooth and light; the eyes sparkling and intense, large and at times dusted with tinges of gold. Under a lunar influence the eyes may not be strong and would therefore have the native donning spectacles at an early age.

This planet if situated in the ascendant signifies beneficial aspects from all standpoints.

Astro Advice

• Worship womanhood or any goddess.
• Avoid alcohol and intoxicants.

The Sun in the Second House

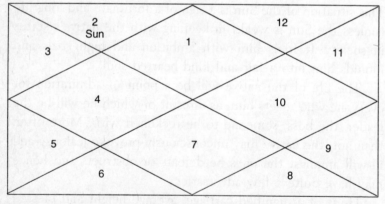

The situation is a beneficial one from the point of view of money matters. It endows the native with a unique value for self, physical qualities rather than actual bravery, self-esteem, an inclination for attractive things as well as a powerful leaning towards luxury and show. If the planet is in a weak sign, like Libra or Aries, the native may well be extravagant and often misinterpreted; if he is an artist or leading an unconventional life, he could live in penury.

Under a good aspect of Venus, this planet symbolises a marriage into a rich family, much higher than the native's present social condition. If it is in a domicile of Mercury, that is, Virgo or Gemini, the alliance will take place for reasons linked with money and not love and affection.

The Sun in the 2nd House forms politicians, bankers, leaders of business and companies.

Astro Advice

- Prayer to Lord Shiva or your Guru will bring good luck.
- Donate red cloth on full and new moon days.

The Sun in the Third House

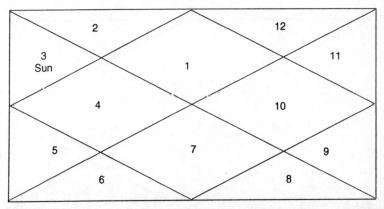

The Sun placed in this position is favourable for the academic pursuits of the native. It offers opportunities for progress and growth through the use of gray cells. He has sound, thorough education with an inclination for everything that is aesthetic and real and which may have use. But more than anything else, he will have a dignity, a grace that will equip him to make a mark in society.

This position also signifies the help of all those who surround the native. This support will be both financial and moral. It makes the native the most significant member of his family. Placed in a watery sign, such as Scorpio, Pisces or Cancer, it represents a great number of trips, mainly for enjoyment and recreation.

Astro Advice

- Favourable direction for *puja* is north-east.
- Wear a gold chain around your neck.

The Sun in the Fourth House

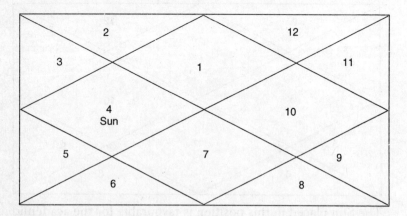

This particular position of the planet endows the native with attachment to the family. It is a definite indicator of a gain in riches as a result of the native's qualities.

It symbolises progress and fortune for the father or through the father. In a horoscope, this position indicates that the child is born of a father who is in a comfortable financial position or who will be able to reach this in the coming times.

This also indicates that the native will have good fortune in his 40th year, which will bring him appreciation and recognition rather than wealth.

If the position is at the nadir, then it is not so beneficial from the health point of view. It causes disorders of the constitution; the native may be fragile and have some serious disorder of the nature of the Sign which is positioned in the 4th House.

From the moral viewpoint, this position often makes the native careful, slightly aloof and curt.

Astro Advice

• Visit a Shiva temple daily and pour milk on 'Shiva-Lingam'.

The Sun in the Fifth House

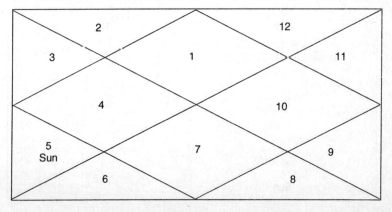

The planet in the 5th House is not beneficial for children, since the Sun is barren. In productive signs (like Cancer, Pisces or Scorpio) it will result in a few children. These children will be of fragile constitution and may die at a young age unless the Moon helps through a favourable aspect.

Placed in this house, the Sun endows a liking for enjoyment or may even force the native to get related to pleasurable activities since he has a polished temperament. He may indulge in a great deal of money-spending. However, this will in no way have an adverse influence on his standing, as the Sun in this position is a beneficial sign always symbolising wealth and a fortunate post. However, it may result in sinful but monetarily rewarding business.

Astro Advice

• Pray to the sun every morning.

The Sun in the Sixth House

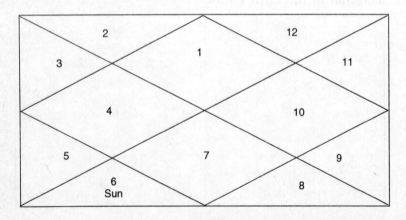

This position may indeed be termed as one of the most unfavourable one for the Sun unless it is highly influential in the sign it is occupying. It bodes ill-health for the native. He will suffer from severe disorders which will threaten his life and hinder him from doing activities which he could have otherwise done.

The planet in this position endows fine skills for organising and planning. Unless it is well aspected, the Sun in the 5th house does not indicate a leader, but one who will progress by virtue of other people.

It always represents fortunate divine assistance in times of trials and tribulations except in health matters.

This position also signifies that the native is blessed with the ability to heal and cure.

Astro Advice

Chant the following *mantra* in the morning for life, light and prosperity:

'Aum Hran Hrin Hron Sae Suryaye Namah.'

The Sun in the Seventh House

This position, like the Sun in the 2nd House, signifies the chance of being married into a high status and rich family, much higher than the native's own. It also indicates a great deal of assistance from the spouse. Therefore, success, wealth and recognition are achieved after getting married.

This is the most favourable position for one who has the desire to enter politics, since it is a definite indicator of

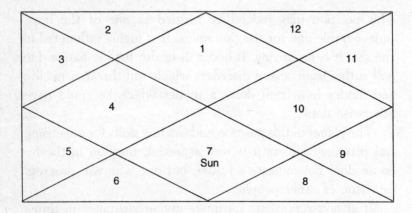

popularity. It always gets a rise at some point in life, and steadiness and security is sure if the planet is influential and aspected well.

This position also signifies a long life and is beneficial for court matters.

The Sun in the 7th House in a marital sign brings discord in the home and is a definite indication of separation or even divorce.

Astro Advice

• Seek the blessings of your parents.

The Sun in the Eighth House

In this position, the planet is an indicator of an unforeseen or traumatic demise around the 50th year as a result of cardiac problems, only if aspects from Saturn and Mars confirm this. In the horoscope of a female, it is an indication that she will lose her husband. It signifies that the father passes away prior

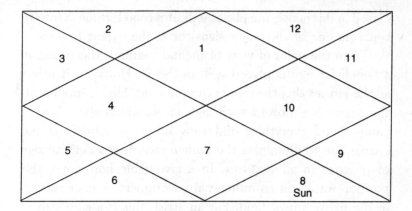

to the mother. This position is beneficial for alliances and matrimony.

Astro Advice

- Ladies can worship Lord Shiva.
- Fast on Sundays.

The Sun in the Ninth House

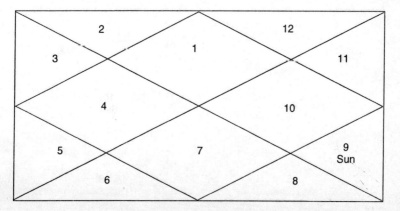

Placed in this house, the planet indicates good fortune in foreign lands (in one of the water signs) or in the export business.

From the point of view of mental faculties, this planet in a beneficial sign is placed well in the 9th House as it offers all the virtues that the mind can ever want. Highly intelligent, the native is endowed with high ideals which allow him to comprehend everything and view life as it actually is and enable him to illuminate the human race. It is a definite sign of progress in all ventures. In a favourable horoscope, this position results in an influential government post or success in the native's own field. For an artist, this is a sure sign of fortune and in all cases, it gives moral peace similar to true happiness and joy.

Astro Advice

• No drinks and a simple diet are suggested.

The Sun in the Tenth House

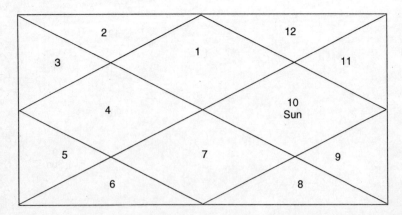

This position is at all times an indication of good fortune and progress at a time close to that of birth. The Sun in the 10th House gets for the native a position higher than the one in which he was born and in keeping with his social standing, his goals and the point from where he started, all of which corresponds to the influence of the 3rd and 4th Houses. His rise to the topmost rung in terms of duties becomes a reality.

This position indicates the help and assistance of the mother or father and dominant female influences. Also it signifies that the native will be highly powerful in his family and will be ready to assist, provided that Venus is aspected well.

Astro Advice

- Chant the following *mantra* 108 times in the morning at 7.00 a.m. after taking bath:
  'Aum Hran Hrin Hron Sai Suryaye Namah.'

The Sun in the Eleventh House

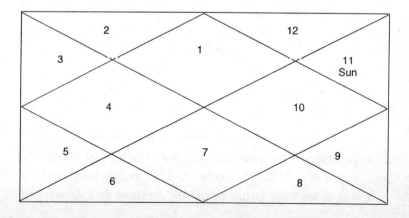

The planet in the 11th House gives the native highly influential friends and acquaintances who will assist him in his profession. If the planet is dignified, it will enable the native to become the chief of a political party or the leader of a school of artists and win a great number of friends. The planet in this position does not favour offsprings – either they will be few or the native will show disinterest in them.

The Sun in the 11th House, if dignified will benefit all alliances. If not, then it will earn strong adversaries, untrue acquaintances and disputes with relations of one's spouse.

Astro Advice

• Donate copper utensils to a temple.

The Sun in the Twelfth House

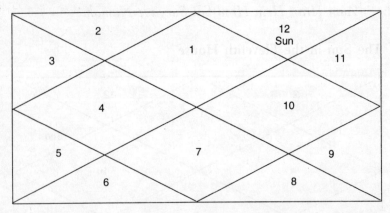

This position of the planet symbolises the idea of seclusion, and a sedate, solitary existence. The native may be in a hospital or nursing home or prison – either as a convict or as a warden (this is applicable to the father or guardian).

If it is badly aspected, such placement signifies estrangement from relations and severe disputes which definitely indicates a life of solitude and loneliness. If aspected well it signifies that the native will conquer difficulties, even though there may be many.

Astro Advice

• Worship Lord Vishnu daily in the morning.

THE SUN IN THE SIGNS

The Sun in Aries

The planet is glorified in the 19th degree of Aries. Placed in this sign, it endows one with an aspiring and somewhat reckless temperament, a varied professional life – one marked by both highs and lows, however, consisting mainly of highs, as whenever he comes down he climbs up higher later in life.

Such a position of the Sun indicates that the native will travel to some place on behalf of someone who belongs to a social stratum higher than the native himself. For an employee, it implies travelling for his boss. For a business person, it denotes travel.

The Sun in 20° of Aries indicates an act of violence, one that will bring dispute and a bad name.

In 10° of Aries, the native will get success, progress and growth, however due efforts must be made or else, he will have to wait long in order to realise this success.

Astro Advice

- Throw four copper coins in flowing water.

The Sun in Taurus

The Sun situated in Taurus does not bode well for marital and home concerns. If Venus is afflicted, it is a definite indicator of severe conflicts and even a separation or divorce. This position does give keen observation and also the ability to keep quiet. It also benefits trips and travel.

The Sun in 10° of Taurus is the creator and instigator of alternation in affections, envious deeds and always signifies an occurrence connected with issues related to the House occupied by the sign. It may result in unfavourable modification.

Placed in 20° of Taurus, it implies sorrow, grief or a daytime trip relating to one's father or spouse. It is therefore related to issues concerned with the house.

Astro Advice

- You must stick to moral values and worship Lord Ganesha.

The Sun in Gemini

The Sun is well placed in Gemini. It indicates a successful profession which is assisted by both acquaintances and relations of the native. It also denotes a hurried trip either by road or by air.

The thoughts and thinking of the native will lean towards logic, criticism and acquiring knowledge. If the Sun is aspected well and not influenced badly by malefic planets, there will be progress in business and mechanical ventures. This is especially so when the Sun is in 20° of Gemini wherein it endows bravery and gentleness which leads to an ascent in life, as the native will be able to enlist support from one and all as a result of his genuinely kind and understanding temperament.

The Sun in 10° of Gemini is not very beneficial since the native is unsure of himself and this results in his passing up several favourable chances. He is fearful and nervous. Still he will get results as a consequence of his pragmatic nature and his determination to finish whatever he starts. In women especially, a Venus or Mars-afflicted Sun results in a undependable and changing temperament.

Astro Advice

- Avoid non-vegetarian food and drinks on Sundays and Thursdays.

The Sun in Cancer

The planet is not very well situated in Cancer. It makes the native lazy or at the very least, dreamy and vague. He is born in a rich family and has a sufficient earning. He will be able to do anything that will do him good. When well-aspected however, this position will be of a high thinker, successful artist or of one fond of beneficial and beautiful things. It leads to a tendency for water travel. Situated in the 3rd House, influenced slightly by Mars – which offers activity – the native may be an energetic rover. In the 9th House, a great deal of journeying by sea is indicated. The Sun in Cancer however gives the native a fragile state of health.

In 10° of Cancer, the Sun may result in a great deal of disputes, arguments and fights and the native may not know how to protect himself from these. Moreover, he will face continuous moral strife which will prevent him from taking any action.

Situated in 20° of Cancer, the placing is more beneficial. Assistance will come from unforseen quarters. In this case, the dark clouds will give way to sunny radiance. Wickedness will disappear and goodness will return.

Astro Advice

- Immerse oil, food-grains or wine (equal to the weight of your body) in flowing water on *Pooranmashi* (full moon day).

The Sun in Leo

Here the Sun is in its own domicile and is therefore very influential. It is also for the native to actualise his wishes provided that the planet is not afflicted by malefic planets. The native has a lot of confidence in himself which will allow him to call upon supportive ideas and therefore, achieve his desire. He is forever correct, his inclination right and his love of beauty and honesty are the usual leading lights. He is gentle yet firm. Those around him must conform to his desires in order to remain acquainted with him. Such a placement frequently depicts several adversaries. However the native will be able to conquer them.

Situated in 10° of Leo, the planet gives the native immense assistance of a loyal acquaintance who will enlist the support of the native's other friends and earn for him a fast climb up the ladder of success.

The Sun in 20° of Leo gives the native ability to avoid all the traps and temptations of life and blesses him with actual influence and strength. The native will actualise his dreams since his dreams will be lofty and demand top priority and he shall gain it as a result of the planet's particular position.

Astro Advice

- Prayer to Sun or Shiva *puja* daily in the morning will bring prosperity.

The Sun in Virgo

Situated in Virgo, the Sun will suffer many restrictions which shall restrain the native. Such a position indicates tension and shadows of problems in his life as well as the tinges of an unclear, unknown fact. Quite often with negative aspects, this position will signify issues which will be difficult to reveal. In certain conditions, especially in the 3rd House it may denote that there will be some questions attached to the birth of the native, while in the 4th House it indicates poor birth.

If aspected well by Uranus the planet will signify the leader of a cult or religious organisation. It shall frequently indicate that the native will head some kind of organisation or free the influence behind the real head.

Situated in 10° of Virgo, the Sun will bring about severe problems in youth. Only if well aspected will it bring prosperity, some time in the 40th year of the native. However for current issues it is always a reason for delays.

In 20° of Virgo, the planet gives personal favours which may not be disclosed especially in monetary issues. If Venus is placed in an influential sign, it denotes a favourable matrimonial alliance frequently with a partner who has some disability which will only restrict the profiteering partner.

Astro Advice

• Donate *gur* or wheat on Sunday mornings.

The Sun in Libra

The Sun placed in Libra makes the native highly impatient and careless with regard to details. He may make errors and rue them later. This is true for marriage wherein he may pursue the flimsy and leave the actual resulting in divorce and separations. In Libra, the Sun is in its fall and brings arguments, court cases, adversaries, moral isolation and even a term in prison. However if, on the whole, the horoscope is beneficial, the foregoing may be evaded since the native is blessed with excellent intellect and brain power.

Situated in 10° of Libra, the Sun with Venus in one of the decanates of Aries, Scorpio or Virgo is a sure indicator of estrangement from one's spouse. In this sign, the Sun if in good aspect with Jupiter, signifies moral uplift of the native, prosperity in his ventures. However at the same time it also indicates desolation since the planet in its fall in the domicile of Venus always withholds love from the native.

The planet in 20° of Libra offers plenty the accomplishment of wishes. However, it also causes stress with reference to offsprings who will move away from the parents. Herein too the planet will bring about estrangement from one's spouse, a vacant, lonely existence and if this is in the 9th House, it will imply breathing one's last in an overseas land.

Astro Advice

- Offer water to sun daily in the morning.
- Give food to five blind persons.

The Sun in Scorpio

This position of the Sun is not at all beneficial. It denotes an advisor who is self-centred and proud. It is not favourable for the health of the native. More so if the planet is in the 6th House since that itself is not beneficial for the planet. It indicates a great deal of fever and frequently diseased blood. If badly aspected by Mars, it is an indication of a violent end, frequently through some mishap. If the Moon is in opposition or conjunction with the planet, it denotes faulty vision.

The native will be very clever because of which he will be able to settle many conflicts with his seniors. Aside from the 6th, 8th and 10th Houses, this planet situated in Scorpio may lead to a temporary betterment in status and also endow the native with life and vigour.

Placed in 10° of Scorpio, the situation is worse and if prosperity is accomplished at a particular point, it may not be as a result of noble work. If Mercury is placed adversely in the horoscope, the position of the Sun in this decanate will denote financial ruin, failure of business ventures which will rob the native of all that he has.

Astro Advice

• Get up early in the morning and seek the blessings of parents after offering water to the rising sun.

The Sun in Sagittarius

The Sun situated in Sagittarius signifies that the native enjoys leading a comfortable and good life. His senses are highlighted more so from the aesthetic viewpoint. His manners are pleasing and he knows how to lead his own life and allows others to lead theirs. Since he is gentle and helpful, people may try to take undue advantage of him. However, he will only gain from this, as even if the planet is adversely aspected, the beneficial deeds done by him shall not be overlooked and he shall be rewarded and assisted when he needs it the most. But since the Sun always gets freedom from tensions and a perpetual growth in this sign, the native will hardly ever need assistance or aid. This situation is favourable for matrimonial alliances. Marriage will take place early, however the union may not always be happy since steadiness is not a characteristic of the

Sun in Sagittarius. It is not beneficial for the offspring, too, as disagreements spring up soon between the husband and wife.

The Sun in 10° of Sagittarius gets quick and easy prosperity, however enjoyment and work may bring certain disturbances in life. If the Sun is not above the horizon, the native may pass away sometime in his fifties.

Situated in 20° of Sagittarius, the mind is simple and self-denying even as it retains its holistic thoughts. It endows plenty of steadiness, good circle of acquaintances, more enthusiasm, less stress on materialism, the ability to perceive beyond the ordinary as well as less of kindness. There will also be greater good fortune in matrimony.

Astro Advice

• Offer milk to a Shivalingam daily.

The Sun in Capricorn

The planet in Capricorn signifies a great deal of vigour, energy and enthusiasm. If the Moon is not placed, then great expenditure of energy may cut life short. The thoughts of the native are complicated, careful and closed and if Jupiter is well aspected, the Sun may bring prosperity.

The planet, when especially in Capricorn, brings disillusionment in matters of the heart and disputes over issues ruled by the house in which this sign is situated.

Placed in 10° of Capricorn, the Sun bestows acute observation and makes the native clever and even cunning –

protecting him from deceit or giving him the ability to detect fraud and cheating so that prosperity and progress are accomplished by virtue of ability, cleverness, care and adeptness.

The Sun in 20° of Capricorn endows the native with strength, resilience and influence. It produces autocratic leaders who get themselves obeyed through force and compulsion. If Mars is well placed in the horoscope, it is a definite indicator of progress in life. However in this decanate, it indicates the native will be alone, mainly due to his severe nature, which will lead to him being feared rather than adored and liked by others.

Astro Advice

• Wear Ruby of 5 carats on the ring finger on a Sunday morning after *Pran Pratishtha*.

The Sun in Aquarius

In this sign, the planet is in exile and hence, loses a great deal of its beneficial qualities from the viewpoint of prosperity since Saturn is stronger over here. If the Sun is badly aspected, it will result in many problems related to issues ruled by the house in which the Sign is situated.

Placed in 10° of Aquarius, the planet brings infidelity, tumultuous disputes with one's spouse, cheating and trickery.

The planet in 20° of Aquarius bestows great mental faculties if Uranus is well placed in the horoscope; otherwise it results in strange thoughts and maybe is the causative factor of madness of the father. In any case, if the Moon is also afflicted it is a sign of peculiarity and oddness.

Astro Advice

- Get up before sunrise.
- Immerse empty vessels after Surya *puja* in flowing water for 90 days.

The Sun in Pisces

The Sun situated in Pisces is not a good token for health. It indicates laziness, hesitation or recklessness and pride.

This placement of the Sun gives the native an unbalanced temperament and a varied life. Great thrift is followed by the desire to splurge and spend to whet unlimited desires and wants.

The native may have a lot of lofty aspirations but no constancy of goals, which often leads to his ruin just when he might have accomplished his goals, unless Mars is placed in Aries.

Despite a fragile state of health, the native has a great number of years to live since he does not use too much of his energy and enthusiasm.

Situated in 10° of Pisces, there might be lack of stability. Life may not have a happy conclusion with a possibility of death through pleurisy. It is not beneficial for matrimony or an offspring who may be rather sensitive and fragile.

The planet in 20° of Pisces endows greater stability and health of the native is slightly better. Death comes late in life and may be through kidney ailments.

Astro Advice

- Wear Ruby of 6 carats on the ring finger on Sunday morning after *Pran Pratishtha*.
- Prayer to Lord Shiva every morning is auspicious.

The Moon

The Moon is damp, cold, constantly changing, feminine and nocturnal. It symbolises materialistic articles. Its domicile is in Cancer, its exaltation at 3 degrees of Taurus and its fall is in Scorpio.

In analysis it should be taken as the Mother. It also signifies night, fortune, hidden and mysterious things, trips, inheritance, moral (rather than physical) mobility.

The native becomes adaptable and fickle, an avid traveller and unable to stay still. If aspected by Uranus, it makes him odd at times.

It bestows him with a nice face and eyes, porcelain skin and a somewhat sluggish constitution. It has greater influence on his brain, bladder, or vision.

It results in ailments of the digestive system, the kidneys, paralysis and also has a great deal of effect on menses and reproduction. It endows a long life and should often be taken as the ruler of life in a horoscope.

It rules the metal silver and its day is Monday. It often symbolises the mother or the wife.

THE MOON IN THE HOUSES

The Moon in the First House

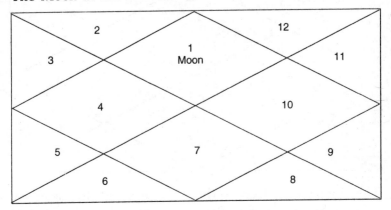

Situated in the 1ˢᵗ House, the Moon makes the native good-natured, creative, versatile, timid, with a tendency to exaggerate little things and also the ability of bearing unpleasant things for a long time till a point when he will simply give up. Though he may not have strong will power, his ability of not yielding is very strong.

In this house, the Moon may make the native prone to alcoholism, more so if the ascendant is in Cancer, Pisces, or Scorpio and if it is in Virgo, Sagittarius or Pisces, then to dreaming and mediumship.

If birth occurs between noon and midnight, it implies a long life.

Astro Advice

• Chant the following *mantra* in the morning:
  'Aum Shran Shrin Shron Chandra Mase Namah.'

The Moon in the Second House

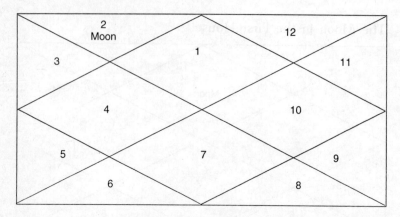

The Moon when placed in the 2ⁿᵈ House, bestows the native with an abundance of profits, good fortune, however marked with rise and falls. If well aspected by Venus, it is beneficial for a wealthy matrimonial alliance or in any case, marriage to one whose financial status is higher than that of the native.

If badly aspected in the 2ⁿᵈ House, it bodes ill for pecuniary issues, since it gets a great deal of indolence, inconstancy and reticence which will make problems of life unconquerable. However if well aspected then it indicates good fortune and none of the aforementioned things will happen.

It signifies a feverish bout at an early age.

Astro Advice

• Donate rice, sugar and milk in temple for seven consecutive Mondays.

The Moon in the Third House

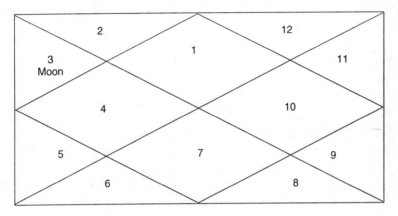

In the 3rd House, the Moon signifies many trips, a highly changeable existence brought about by the native himself due to his mind always being affected by the one with whom he interacted last, though this does not stop him from doing whatever he wishes to do prior to anything else.

He has a fertile imagination and an inclination for literary and artistic pursuits. However, his intellect is not very great since the mind is lazy.

The native will have a disposition to change his mind all of a sudden. His ability to memorise and retain will be good, and more so his visual memory. In this house, the Moon symbolises hidden or mysterious things in the family.

Astro Advice

- Give food to black crows daily.
- Bathe with cow's milk for five Mondays.

The Moon in the Fourth House

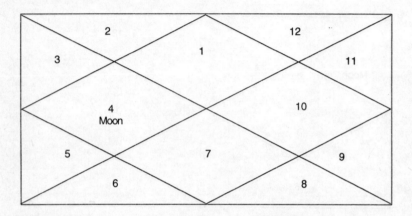

The Moon situated in the 4th House symbolises pleasant home environs, however lacking material solidity, since the home will be disorganised and shall witness many modifications.

The early stages of life will not be very lucky; however betterment takes place and the last stage improves.

Vague and shadowy events will take place in relation to death and legacies. Problems will crop up in connection with estates and property.

In the 4th house, the Moon is beneficial for the native's mother. However, if the Sun, which symbolises the father, is in Aquarius or Libra then she may become a widow.

Astro Advice

- Donate milk, rice or silver to a Brahmin.
- Ladies can worship *Panchamukha deepam*.

The Moon in the Fifth House

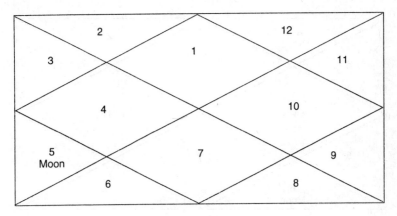

The Moon in this house bestows the native with an inclination towards sensuality, excess enjoyment and makes him changeable in matters of the heart. There exists a possibility of a number of offsprings in fruitful signs such as Pisces, Cancer or Scorpio.

The native dislikes loneliness and indulges in reckless spending, such as speculation, betting, gambling.

Since the native is able to get what he wants with great ease and is exceedingly fortunate, he may get indolent. If well aspected, it provides an inclination for drama and gets prosperity in love, politics and arts.

This situation makes the native lively and enthusiastic. He is blessed with friends and is also popular.

Astro Advice

- Those suffering from witchcraft should take a bath with cow's urine on a full moon day.
- Prayer to Lord Shiva is appropriate.

The Moon in the Sixth House

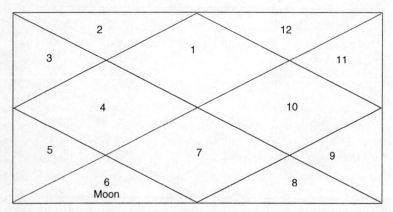

Placed in the 6th House the Moon does not make a leader or head, rather such a situation makes the native a servant of morality or materialism, irrespective of what his social standing may be. It gives prosperity only in junior and lower positions and signifies a worker who completes a hidden or unacknowledged task.

For a female, this symbolises threat in childbirth and stomach ailments, while for a male, it represents urinary complaints, more so if there is an evil aspect between Saturn and Mars in Sagittarius or Scorpio, in which case surgery may be required.

The Moon placed in the 6th House, invariably puts pressure on the native's health.

Astro Advice

• While sleeping place a glass full of water on your bedside and pour it on Arabica (*kekar*) in the morning.

The Moon in the Seventh House

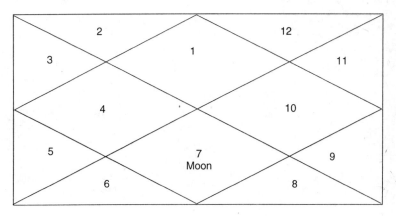

From the point of view of marriage, the effect of the Moon will be akin to the one in the 2ⁿᵈ House. However it will be of a superior and higher state. The union will be happy in accord and balance and lucky. But the Moon should not get any bad aspects from Saturn or Uranus.

This placement of the Moon is highly beneficial for court cases. If in adverse aspect with Venus it may cause change in affection if cards signifying infidelity are drawn. However, it does not destroy the home. Situated in the 7ᵗʰ House, the Moon causes problems for the mother or wife.

Astro Advice

- Your favourable direction for *puja* is north-west.
- Offer seven types of foodgrains equal to the weight of your body to roadside wanderers.

The Moon in the Eighth House

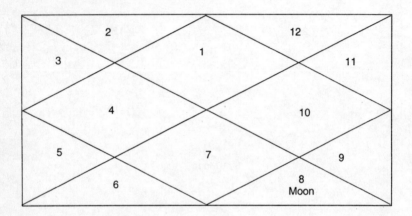

The Moon placed in the 8th House, in the case of a man, may make him lose his wife to death. If well aspected by the Sun, it implies the passing away of the mother. It also indicates the inheritance of money.

Very serious danger is signified for the mother who may ail from kidney problems. If in adverse aspect with Mars, it indicates an attack of uraemia on the mother resulting in a quick death.

It also signifies disputes with female relations, which may even involve physical manhandling and abuse.

Astro Advice

- Full and new moon days or Mondays are good for fasting.
- Must offer rice, silver, coins, wheat, milk in *Tula-Daan*.

The Moon in the Ninth House

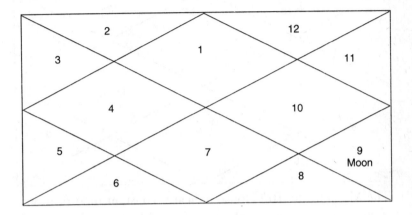

When situated in the 9th House, the Moon always represents long trips, generally crossing water bodies and relating to financial matters. It gives an inclination to spirituality, dreams and clairvoyance. It is quite alike to the situation in the 1st House; however it has greater hold over the mind than the body and hence endows the native with imaginary, fickle thoughts, somewhat prone to unconscious lying. At times it may bring about anomalies in the brain (mad or brilliant) depending upon the beneficial or adverse aspects received by the Moon. Moreover if the Moon is placed badly or afflicted by Mars and Saturn, travelling may be endangered.

Astro Advice

• Bathe with cow's milk or curd.

The Moon in the Tenth House

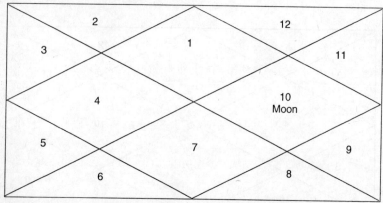

The Moon in the 10th House indicates constant modifications with reference to material status. If the Moon is well aspected these alterations shall be very lucky. This position bestows unforeseen prosperity and popularity. The Moon in this house gives the very best to all those who wish to be in the limelight such as actors, politicians and others.

It represents that the native shall be assisted in his professional climb by a woman and he shall rise very fast. It also signifies that sale or purchase of a house shall yield great profits.

Astro Advice

• Give *gur* to the blind for 21 Mondays.

The Moon in the Eleventh House

Placed in the 11th House, the Moon gives the native a lot of female acquaintances as well as the support and shelter of powerful ladies.

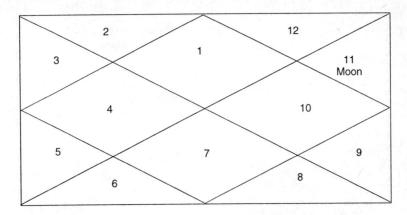

The friend circle is wide and relations keep changing and are artificial. It always signifies a large family, especially girls in a woman's horoscope and boys in that of a man.

It represents that the native shall receive awards, recognition and approval amongst his friends. This may be temporary and occur again. Prosperity will take place in large organisations. The situation is beneficial for administrative positions. It also signifies trips with one's acquaintances.

There may be some legal fight with a person who does business in water or other liquids.

Astro Advice

- Avoid non-vegetarian food and drinks.
- Wear cat's eye on ring finger on Monday morning after *pran pratishtha*.

The Moon in the Twelfth House

This position of the Moon symbolises peace, calm and quiet in the home environment. It also signifies benevolence and

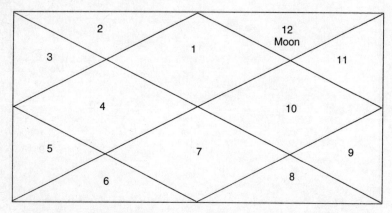

implies sacrificing one's own desires for the sake of others. This position is found in gentle souls, nurses, loyal women and good samaritans.

In case the Moon is weak or adversely aspected in the house, there will be strange problems or occurrences in life. In Gemini or Virgo especially there will be nervous disorders, hysteria in Capricorn, enmities in Aries, convulsion in Scorpio, sleep walking in Taurus; all of these occur due to women – a mother, wife or lover. It represents genuine or imagined betrayal since in the 12th House it signifies a persecution mania, especially if Saturn or Mars are situated in unfavourable signs and are also adversely aspected with the Moon.

Astro Advice

- Donate white articles like milk, sugar or cloth to a poor man.

MOON IN THE SIGNS

The Moon in Aries

Situated in Aries, the Moon endows the native with a highly

fertile imagination, a temperament that varies constantly and an inclination to look at life from an imaginative point of view. It also makes him strange, restless and somewhat unsure of himself. This position forms writers, poets and lawyers. It holds the possibility of second sight, causes sudden, reckless journeys by sea and gives more force of inertia rather than actual determination and perseverance.

In 10° of Aries, the Moon will get unforeseen fortune which will enable the native to release himself from problems.

In 20° of Aries, it is unlucky for almost every single thing since there is a deficiency of organising skills and bravery. This is an unfortunate situation.

When the Moon is placed in this sign, particularly at 20° of Aries, the native may be prone to a face or head injury.

Astro Advice

- Prayer to the Moon daily in the morning is a must which will bestow light, positive thinking and prosperity.

The Moon in Taurus

The Moon placed in Taurus is fortunate on the whole but more so in matters of love and affection and financial issues. It makes the native soft, slightly delicate, understanding and his disposition prompts him to search for calm and quiet and go for strolls by the lake or sea. The voice of the native sounds soothing to the ears, however it may be spoilt early in life and there may be chances of throat problems.

Situated in 10° of Taurus, the Moon shows inconstancy, infidelity or envy. However, the native will profit by these.

In 20° of Taurus, the Moon invariably signifies travel, however there could be problems. It also signifies changes and modifications in matters of love.

Placed in Taurus, the Moon is a definite indicator of prosperity for artists.

Astro Advice

- Avoid drinks and non-vegetarian food.
- Worship Maa Durga.

The Moon in Gemini

The Moon situated in Gemini signifies carelessness and rash deeds, and frequent idle, meaningless chatter. It bestows the native with great intelligence and he is inclined towards the academic pursuit of literature, history and geography. Numerous short trips will occur. Life will be long but interrupted by several disputes, despite the native's desire for peace and quiet.

In 10° of Gemini, it indicates unfaithfulness to someone who is close to the native, frequently a relative.

Situated in 20° of Gemini it brings a great number of educated acquaintances who shall enable the native to progress and grow.

Astro Advice

- Donate seven grains in a temple.
- Wear cat's eye of six *rattis* on a Monday.

The Moon in Cancer

Herein the Moon is situated in its own domicile. It endows immense sensitivity. There is a yearning for short trips and travel. However, the native shall always come back to his home which he holds most dear. The native's mental powers are strong. His scrupulous and open temperament make him vulnerable to deceit. It endows him with a strong mind and body, only if not ill-influenced by Saturn or Mars, as an adverse influence from those two results in lymphatism or lung problems.

Well aspected by Jupiter, it ensures definite growth. However placed in 10° of Cancer, this will be difficult since there may be unforeseen hindrances by Saturn. Also there will be threats of mishaps when on a journey and though they may not be grave yet they will cause tiredness and tensions.

In 20° of Cancer the native will have some violent deed committed against him and he shall be surrounded by problems. However, assistance and relief will come to him from a female, usually mother or spouse.

Astro Advice

• Wear *Chandra Yantra* of eight metals around the neck.

The Moon in Leo

Situated in Leo, the Moon endows and blesses with the very best. Success and growth are certain in a professional or academic line. It creates the writer, the scientist, the musician, the poet. It showers determination, aspirations and hard work. The temperament is blunt, egoistic and vain. The mind is artificial but there is a fondness for the home and offspring.

Since energy and vitality are high, the native may at times take on more than he can handle. However if well aspected by Mars and particularly by Moon in 20° of Leo, he shall be able to prosper through hardship by virtue of his hard work and determination.

Placed in Leo the Moon can cause poor vision and force the native to start wearing spectacles at an early age.

In 10° of Leo, it signifies fidelity and inclination to be overly trusting of one and all.

In 20° of Leo, it brings ailments of the heart while in 20° of Leo it results in blood poisoning, if the Sun in the horoscope is adversely situated.

Astro Advice

• Help a widow.
• Give foodgrain to birds.

The Moon in Virgo

When placed in this sign, the Moon gives the native an odd temperament. His mind shall be highly perceptive and this will allow him to prosper in the occult world. It will give him the inclination to dream, to use the second sight, and to attain enlightenment. He will commit errors as a result of lack of logic and experience. If adversely aspected by Mars, he shall not be hard working.

The wicked effect of Saturn will result in severe digestive ailments. This situation will cause the gravest stomach problems in females, often making them barren. Despite the disorders, the Moon endows the native with a long life. Marriage is more based on emotions rather then fortune.

In 10° of Virgo the Moon is unlucky from the materialistic viewpoint. It will always result in postponement of the native's plans and their actualisation and he may do things which shall fail since they will lack a solid base.

In 20° of Virgo, if Venus is placed well, there will be a rich marriage and the union will be balanced and in harmony since the Moon in Virgo shall enable the native to bear with the shortcomings of the spouse.

Astro Advice

* Donate white cloth to a sweeper.
* Immerse four square pieces of silver in flowing water.

The Moon in Libra

The Moon situated in Libra gets numerous legal issues or a profession that will involve dealing with police, lawyers etc.

The native has a direct, candid and dutiful mind but is slightly reticent. Everything about him is dignified and cultured including his attire which exudes austerity. Happiness and an ever present wish for recreation will prompt him to enjoy the company of people younger to him.

Logic and pragmatism characterise him and his clear and fertile imagination make him a fluent speaker, one who does not digress from the main topic.

In 10° of Libra, the situation creates successful political figures.

The Moon is beneficial in 20° of Libra also, and bestows great growth only if there is no adverse aspect of Mars. In that case, it will result in an unforeseen but temporary throwback since the native will be able to retrieve the glorified position he rightfully holds.

Astro Advice

- Donate milk in Bhairo Mandir.
- Wear Pearl of four *rattis*.

The Moon in Scorpio

The Moon is at its fall in 3° of Scorpio and hence is highly unlucky for all issues ruled by the Moon. It creates a tendency towards perjury and robs the native of any good attributes. He cannot shake off his inner inclinations towards deceit, indolence or excessiveness. These may be attired by favourable influences. However there shall be too many problems to conquer, ill-luck and a life marked with diseases and threats of all types.

Such a situation is not good for childbirth and also signifies barrenness, at time miscarriages, provided Mars is weak.

In 20° of Scorpio, it signifies either an untruthful deed committed by a woman or a dishonest act that harms one.

If the Moon while in Scorpio is adversely aspected by Mars or Saturn and is placed in the 8th House it indicates that the native shall suffer bereavement.

Astro Advice

- Recite the Gayatri *Mantra*.
- Give sweets to girls.

The Moon in Sagittarius

Situated in Sagittarius, the Moon signifies an unworldly mind, idealism and carelessness with respect to attire. It signifies a disregard for finances and wealth. However, the native will never lack these since the Moon frequently gets legacies while in the Sign. Prosperity is indicated through the wife who shall help her partner morally, financially and mentally. There may be hardship and strenuous labour, however, the desired destination shall always be reached. The Moon in Sagittarius, gives a big and harmonious domestic circle.

Situated in 10° of Sagittarius, the Moon gets numerous alterations with regards to the native's standing in life and society and whatever is started succeeds and prospers.

In 20° of Sagittarius, the Moon bestows great confidence, excellent ability to reach the divine and a tendency to conserve which enables the native to live a long life, particularly if the sign is in the 2nd, 3rd, 5th or 11th House. In the case of angular houses, life may be of a shorter duration.

Astro Advice

- Give gifts to your wife.
- Always speak the truth.

The Moon in Capricorn

The Moon situated in Capricorn, is also an unfortunate position since it signifies an unscrupulous, hypocritical, immoral native (unless aspects are good). It indicates physical and moral slothfulness. The native is reticent and cannot opt between good and evil and generally takes the evil, thereby going further down. Temperamentally, he is depressed, vindictive and not at all pleasant.

The Moon in 10° of Capricorn brings transient prosperity which is always followed by ruin. Women are the cause for great worry and marriage is also not very favourable. With an adverse influence of Mercury, threats of cheating, fraud, bankruptcy or any other dishonourable act hangs over the native. A favourable aspect of Jupiter may completely change the aforementioned. However health will not be good and the mind shall be troubled.

In 20° of Capricorn, it brings slightly improved health, provided Mars is influential. However, it signifies a violent end if Capricorn is in the 8th House. The peril shall occur in an alien country and probably during a brief trip.

Astro Advice

- Avoid taking gifts from a widow.
- Provide all comforts to your wife.

The Moon in Aquarius

Situated in Aquarius, the Moon bestows a melancholy, profound and sombre temperament. The native enjoys being by himself and is generally compassionate. However, life's disillusionments may make him distressful of mankind.

This placement brings about an inclination to carry out impossible and impractical, idealistic inquiries which may bring about misfortune. The preference and thoughts of the native are strange, more so if Saturn is badly aspected in which case, the mental state of the native may cause worry.

When influenced in a beneficial manner, the Moon in Aquarius endows the native with an imagination that runs in wild and depressive directions. If his life is morose and morbid it will be his own doing.

However, in spite of all this, this situation of the Moon brings appreciation from the female sex, especially when in 20° of Aquarius. However these alliances will be temporary, strange and ill-matched.

When in 10° of Aquarius it signifies disloyalty, cheating and betrayal of trust in amorous affairs.

Astro Advice

- Recite the Durga *Saptshati*.
- Wear a silver bangle weighing 20 grams.

The Moon in Pisces

Placed in Pisces, the Moon brings a craving for ease and luxury, laziness and a creative imagination, a whole lot of schemes but few implementations. It signifies indecisiveness and changeability in love, with greater appeal to the senses, and less of life and energy. The Moon's placement results in the native being a chatterbox who either defames other people or is himself subject to defamation. He may either cheat others or be cheated himself. It signifies disloyalty, two or more marriages, ill luck in finance related issues, however no penury.

In 10° of Pisces, the Moon signifies a native who lies without realising it and who convinces himself that what he states is true and therefore harms himself more by doing so. Though in these degrees, the Moon has greater energy and life, it is also a definite indicator of unfaithfulness in matrimony.

When in 20° of Pisces if the horoscope is good, the situation of the Moon is highly beneficial as it lets whatever is happening go on in an uninterrupted manner. However in case the horoscope is bad, it will imply the converse.

Note: The placement of the Moon in a horoscope is highly significant and should be analysed both with reference to aspect and position in the house and sign so that an exact judgement may be pronounced.

Astro Advice

- Wear silver ring on the ring finger.
- Feed bananas to monkeys.

Mercury

The planet Mercury is mind-based, arid, nervous and adaptable in the sense that it is changed greatly both by its placements and the aspects received by it. Its exile is in Pisces and Sagittarius. Its day house is in Gemini and night house is in Virgo.

It is favourable for matters related to knowledge and merits extra attention so that the native's mentality may be ascertained.

Mercury holds particular effect on medicine, speech, writing, letters and trade and business. It also stands for pragmatism and is related to property and therefore, wealth. It governs the metal quicksilver.

The planet represents vigour, vitality, happiness, activity, dancing, walking, youth and the child. If influenced adversely, it signifies perjury, deceit and cheating.

Mercury's colour is pale grey and its day is Wednesday.

It signifies a native who is humorous, likes to equivocate, is less artificial and more analytical. He gesticulates a great deal and makes good use of his slender, fragile hands. With an agile and flexible body, his stature is generally short, his nose long and thin, forehead high.

Mercury rules all nervous ailments.

MERCURY IN THE HOUSES

Mercury in the First House

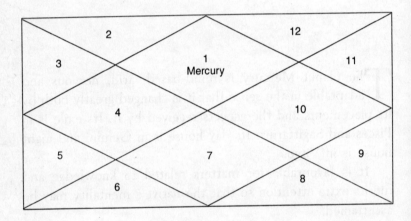

Situated in the 1ˢᵗ House, Mercury bestows a number of moral qualities on the native – liveliness, an analytical brain, retentiveness, slightly argumentative and meticulous. Such a situation provides success in small enterprises rather than in bigger ones. The native will succeed in a number of small ventures than in a single big one. When situated in this House, Mercury brings pragmatism of mind which enables one to view reality in everything – people, objects, life in general. It represents balance and accord of the mind provided there are no wicked aspects.

Astro Advice

- Throw four copper coins in flowing water.
- Wear *Panna* of five carats on Wednesday on the little finger after *Pran Pratishtha*.

Mercury in the Second House

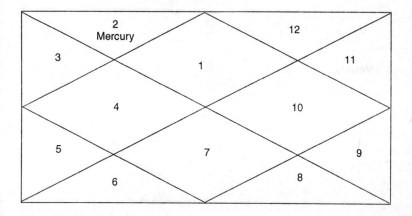

Mercury in the 2nd House is overall a favourable position. With regard to the sale of moveable property placed in this house, it endows the native with a talent for financial issues and gives him the ability to get more wealth by virtue of his inherent talent. Favourably influenced by Venus, it signifies a marriage into a rich family with a mate who is at a good rank and who the native has enticed more by aiming than affecting. Therefore, such a marriage may not always live up to exceptions. In this House, in square with Mars or Venus, Mercury indicates estrangement, infidelity or two or more marriages.

- Give the first bite of your food to a cow.
- Wear copper coin in a black thread.

Mercury in the Third House

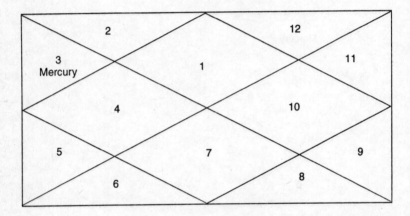

When situated in the 3rd House, Mercury is favourable for academic pursuits. The native shall have the ability to mould himself to both the good and bad aspects of life. He is intelligent as well as capable, and has a liking for learning and literature. This also endows him with a preference for harmony in music rather than for tune.

If influenced beneficially, it is highly beneficial for siblings. The planet generally makes the native either the eldest or the youngest but never the middle one.

It is also good for a number of speedy trips and bestows a deep liking for driving, flying, dancing and walking.

Astro Advice

- Donate *saboot Moong* in a temple.
- Give eatables to crows on Wednesdays.

Mercury in the Fourth House

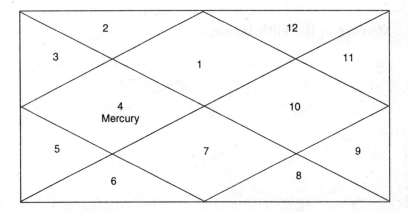

Mercury in the 4th House, when dignified, bestows a happy domestic scenario amid many youthful people, a lot of wealth and cordiality with the in-laws.

However, if the influence is not beneficial then there shall be a lot of squabbling, discord with neighbours and greed. It is highly beneficial for all mental pursuits. Mercury in the nadir leads to a tendency to peruse mathematics and the occult. It indicates a man who sees and notices, who remains quiet, yet who takes decisive and precise action which best suit his motives. The planet's situation in this House is not highly influential. However, it is beneficial for land or domestic property dealings.

This is also an indication of a lack of stability in the home. It is the place of an official who shifts home frequently.

Astro Advice

- Offer grains to the blind.
- Avoid non-vegetarian food.

Mercury in the Fifth House

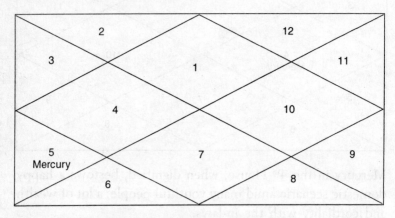

Placed in the 5th House, Mercury is beneficial for monetary matters so long as it is not adversely aspected by Saturn or Mars. When situated in this House, which is related to enjoyment it makes this enjoyment more intellectual and less sensuous. It endows prosperity in mental recreation – drama, concerts, art – more so if Sun and Venus are dignified.

This situation of Mercury is not favourable for offsprings. It gives a small family and causes problems and anxieties related to children. It usually gives an inclination towards bachelorhood or spinsterhood. There may be a number of temporary, short-lived affairs of the heart, but all marked by inconstancy.

Astro Advice

- Recite the following *mantra* 108 times daily:
  '*Aum Bran Bron Sai Budhaye Namah.*'

Mercury in the Sixth House

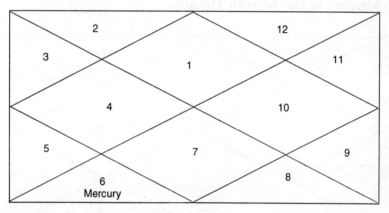

As is the case with every other planet situated in the 6th House, Mercury, too, will be unfavourable for health matters and shall cause ailments relating to the nervous system, chest and intestines. Travel may have to be undertaken because of health problems.

However, when dignified, Mercury in the 6th House is beneficial for junior staff or servants who shall be dedicated and loyal to their employers or seniors. But, with a wicked influence it implies small burglaries committed by the workers.

The planet situated in this House does not create a favourable boss (unless favourably aspected). The native does not have the ability to take decisive actions and does better when working along with or under other people.

Astro Advice

- Donate green vegetables in a temple on Wednesday.
- Chanting of Gayatri *Mantra* or Satyanaryana *Puja* is beneficial.

Mercury in the Seventh House

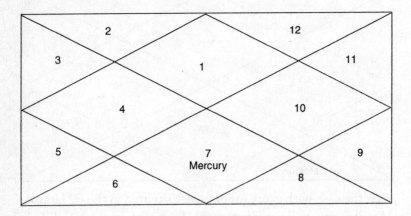

Placed in the 7th House, Mercury is responsible for making the native marry a mate who will be either very youthful-looking or be actually much younger than the native himself. He shall be cultured, intelligent, talkative, dark, short in height and have a flair for oration, medicine and trade.

This position is not beneficial for marriage. There will be disputes, arguments and frequently, a court case which results in estrangement.

On the contrary, it is favourable for trade alliances. It will enable the native to emerge victorious in court cases which shall favour him.

If aspected adversely, Mercury will cause deceit by partners and there is a possibility of downfalls by their own hand. If Saturn is in the 12th House, then there are chances of being locked up in prison as a result of financial ruin.

Astro Advice

- Offer *ghee*, green clothes or utensils at the place of worship on Wednesday evening.

Mercury in the Eighth House

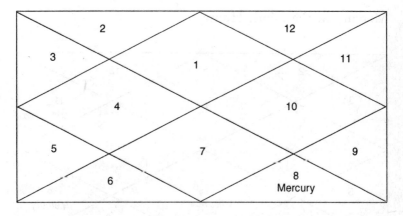

This is a situation that favours matrimony. It indicates, particularly, a mate who will be wealthy and mature in age than the native and so the latter shall inherit legacies.

When badly aspected, the planet causes arguments. Harsh words shall be exchanged in relation to a death and frequently implies the appropriation of legacies. The wicked influence of Mercury in the 8th House shall be the reason of many ailments and often makes the native morose and depressed. With an ill influence of the Moon and with Mercury with Cancer in the 8th House, it may happen that either the native or one of his offsprings is mentally sick or retarded.

When dignified, the planet brings prosperity in the field of writing. In a good horoscope, it indicates that the native shall be applauded and awarded after his demise.

Astro Advice

- Recite Laxmi *Stotra* in the morning.
- Donate water tankers in a religious place.

Mercury in the Ninth House

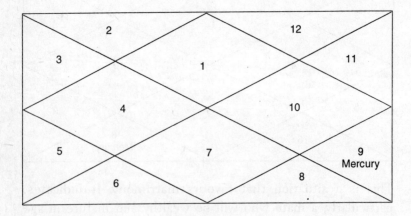

It is a highly beneficial position for mental pursuits. When dignified, Mercury in this House, signifies a high degree of intelligence and the definite assurance of prosperity in all the endeavours of the native due to his excellent intellect. The native is highly intuitive and will immerse himself in the perusal of philosophy or theology. This placement in trine (120°) with the ascendant is beneficial to the native who will absorb Mercury's attributes.

In this House, Mercury brings a number of long trips. It is a favourable placement for people who interact with foreigners and bestows a natural flair for foreign languages.

In a lay out of cards, it signifies that one or more of the native's offspring shall leave for land overseas wherein they shall build their wealth easily.

Astro Advice

• Donate books to poor students.

Mercury in the Tenth House

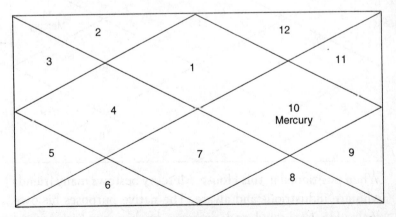

Placed in the 10th House, the planet indicates a native who will be engaged in trade or an academic profession and signifies that children should be instructed on a similar pattern so long as the 5th House is in favourable aspect with the 10th. This situation is beneficial for friends who shall be many and smart. It is beneficial also for social status since it will help the native to earn wealth by virtue of his own attributes. If Mercury is adversely aspected, it signifies inadequacy or uselessness. This position endows many innovative thoughts, however, if Mercury is weak the native shall be an innovator who shall not gain from his work himself but will make other people profit.

Astro Advice

• Donate food grains or gold to a goddess.

Mercury in the Eleventh House

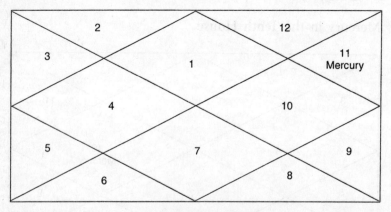

When positioned in this House, Mercury bestows many friends who are industrious and aware. The native purposes his own goals. He is shrewd and prospers by his own virtues and strengths.

This is a beneficial House for the offspring who shall be intelligent and who will go on to assist the father.

Not a favourable position for matters of the heart. The planet makes the native highly changeable but keeps the domestic life intact. The native interacts and mingles easily and is fond of dancing, society and drama.

Adversely aspected, particularly with Mars, the planet result in disputes with progeny, business partners, debates, *et al*.

Astro Advice

* Donate a goat to a poor person.
* Worship Maa Durga.

Mercury in the Twelfth House

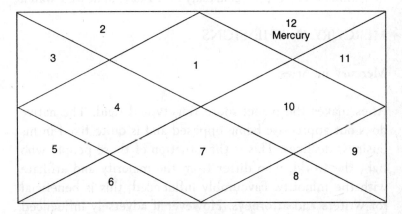

Always unlucky, the 12th House makes no exception for Mercury particularly in Taurus, Capricorn or Scorpio, in which it brings disillusionments relating to the sign. When dignified, it might, because of close proximity to the ascendant and its mobility, justify the prophecy of good luck relating to issues within its sphere: business profits, intelligence, wealth and fluency of speech. But it must be very strong in the horoscope and completely free from any bad aspects since then it would be an omen of uselessness and all ventures shall fail just when success seems certain.

If aspected adversely, it is not beneficial for the progeny who shall be brought up in strange or peculiar circumstances. With a bad aspect from Venus, it shall not be beneficial for feelings and signifies a predisposition for cerebral ailments due to overindulgence.

Astro Advice

•   Immerse one copper coin daily for 21 days in flowing water.

MERCURY IN THE SIGNS

Mercury in Aries

Aries makes the planet more fidgety and rigid. The native does not appreciate being opposed and is quite fixed in his business dealings. This is the situation of those people who fight the world, who differ from the majority and affiliate with the minority. Favourably influenced, this is beneficial for writers and attorneys. However if adversely influenced by the Moon, it leads to perjury. When with a good aspect, the native has acute thinking processes, a clever, sharp mind or enough abilities so as to disentangle himself from his problems, which may be many since he will be amid numerous adversaries.

When in 10° of Aries, the planet indicates a great deal of travelling marked by hardships. Nonetheless, a favourable aspect of the Sun will make these trips beneficial and often, the native will get what his heart desires.

When in 20° of Aries, Mercury brings severe threats in materialistic matters. Also, it is an indication of nervous depression because of fate which the native cannot evade. There may also exist the chances of contracting nervous ailments or typhoid at an early age.

Astro Advice

- Give food to a brown cow.
- Donate green bangles to seven women.

Mercury in Taurus

The planet situated in Taurus has a beneficial effect on the native who is endowed with a happy temperament and an attractive bearing. He is appreciated by people around him and has the chance of entering into a financially fortunate matrimonial alliance.

This situation is favourable for issues related to love and likings. It is a sign of distinct self-centredness. The native will pursue his own enjoyment neglecting his partner. It is beneficial for creative endeavours. These enable the native to make a great deal of profit and gain, since his own benefit is of immense importance to him. He would choose financial gain now rather than posthumous recognition. The planet in Taurus gives him the possibility of making money without any difficulty.

Mercury in 10° of Taurus, signifies a lot of envy, resulting from the mistakes of the native himself. Hardships shall raise their head and growth may be hampered. This situation indicates a total alteration in the status or profession at a particular point in the life of the native.

When in 20° of Taurus, unless very well aspected, the native is not stable or settled and is also the indication of expensive, unprepared travel. When in the 7th House, this situation brings about sadness or anxiety in marriage.

Astro Advice

- Immerse *sarson* in flowing water.
- Put *Moong dal* in a vessel and bury it in a graveyard.

Mercury in Gemini

Mercury situated in Gemini is a beneficial situation from the mental point of view. Since the planet is situated in its own domicile and is very influential, it endows many benefits with reference to the house it is situated in. If situated in the 10th House, it will lead to prosperity. The native is genuinely sympathetic and understanding and shall have the ability to make a number of acquaintances who shall help him as per the aspects the planet receives from other beneficial planets and also, the Houses which they occupy.

When in 10° of Gemini, the planet benefits mental process, however, disposition is fragile. There is a possibility of the native being unnecessarily anxious and creating fictitious problems. He will be over-sensitive and sentimental and will react to things which others may not notice and will therefore, suffer. His acute extra-sensory perception will allow him to plan for the future. Endowed with an academic brain, he shall create a niche for himself depending upon the education he receives.

When in 20° of Gemini, Mercury is suitably positioned. It gives the native the ability to prosper by virtue of his intellect. His gentle and kind nature is a part of Jupiter's nature and a favourable aspect from Mars shall help him succeed.

Astro Advice

• Prayer to Lord Hanuman is beneficial.

Mercury in Cancer

When Mercury is situated in Cancer the planet brings imagination, dreams and journeys. The native may be quite fortunate under this position as such he would be fond of swimming, travelling, mountaineering. The position promises all safety from drowning or accident. It is favourable for persons who are inclined towards mysticism, occultism and spiritualism. It also guards against witchcraft. In certain cases this position is favourable for future events as such the native gains full strength after heartaches and disappointments. The native can be a social worker or leader with a self sacrificing disposition.

Astro Advice

- Offer food- grains, blankets and oil in charity on Saturday evening.
- Ring of five metals like, gold, silver, copper, *kansa* and iron will increase your personal magnetism.

Mercury in Leo

When situated in Leo, the planet brings powerful acquaintances and provided that the 9th House is well disposed, the native might attain the status of a prosperous trader, or even a diplomat or an ambassador. A favourable influence, it makes the native talented, generous, steady, ambitious, reliable and a high thinker. He will have a talent for artistic pursuits and provided that education indicates it, he might prosper in this field. This particular situation also gets prosperity in any venture related to luxury items. The native is endowed with excellent oratory skills and shall, with the assistance of favourable aspects from benefic planets, flourish in any field. Mercury in Leo, in the 5th House, may make the native a famed artist or musician, theatre or entertainment manager.

When in 10° of Leo, if the sign is in the 10th House, Mercury can make the native a simple chatter-box. It brings strong retention, he need not be necessarily a leader but a loyal worker who shall be of immense assistance to his master, if allowed to use his own resourcefulness.

When in 20° of Leo, the planet causes numerous small hardships which shall bring problems related to issues ruled by the house in which the sign is placed; in the 6th House there might be bowel ailments and the threat of auto-toxemia if Mars radiates an adverse aspect; in the 2nd House, it signifies misunderstood individuals or unlucky innovators.

Astro Advice

• Seek the blessings of your elders daily.

Mercury in Virgo

When situated in its own domicile, Mercury is highly beneficial for mental matters, since it makes the mind idealistic, however, slightly logical which makes the native give great weight to minor issues. The mind is fond of debate, particularly if aspected with Mars. However, though it is superior, it does not give great results. It has a preference for subjects relating to philosophy, occult or theology, all of which have no great wealth potential, therefore, the native will not be wealthy. He shall be respected and renowned, however will not be rich. This is a favourable situation for the professor or scientist but not so for someone into business or banking and finance. But if other positions and favourable aspects do the opposite, then these individuals shall rise to great heights.

When situated in 10° of Virgo, Mercury brings many postponements in growth. It brings appreciation and admiration, however no material assistance. It also signifies schemes that help others a great deal.

Placed in 20° of Virgo, the planet is responsible for prosperity with the aid of a female. The native's high mentality may attract a rich woman who may either become his wife or who will definitely give him financial aid to actualise his high ambitions. However, in order for this to occur, Venus and the Moon must be dignified and the planet should not be adversely affected by Uranus or Saturn.

Astro Advice

- Immerse 101 betel leaves in flowing water.

Mercury in Libra

Mercury when situated in Libra signifies a high probability of court cases or quarrels with lawyers. If the planet is well dignified and favourably aspected, it will get profits through these cases however, if this is not so, it shall result in problems, losses and fights, particularly so in the Twelfth House.

Favourably aspected, Mercury placed in Libra bestows a love for one's offspring, beneficial alliances, gainful contracts and investments. This situation is also beneficial for politicians since it brings quick growth. Adversely positioned and affected by unfavourable planets, Mercury results in disillusionment in relation to issues ruled by the house in which the sign is placed.

When placed in 10° of Libra, the planet is highly beneficial for the mind. It is a definite indicator of a well-developed mind and of prosperity as long as there are no adverse aspects. This situation is favourable for academic pursuits and in the 9th House, it gives the native the ability to study foreign languages which shall have a good effect on his status.

When in 20° of Libra, Mercury brings an honourable post, however it is not beneficial for offsprings since they shall cause

great stress. If Mars has an adverse aspect in Mercury in 20°
of Libra and the sign is in the 5th House, then there lies the
threat of the child's early death.

Astro Advice

- Keep a small piece of green cloth in your pocket.
- Touch the feet of your daughter (if below 12 years) or
  worship Maa Durga.

Mercury in Scorpio

When situated in Scorpio, Mercury results in threatening
situations with violent individuals, or serious disputes over
issues related with the House in which this sign is placed. A
wicked aspect of Venus results in disloyalty or cheating in love
with the possibility of estrangement from the spouse. The
native is somewhat vehement as well as cunning. The effect
of Mars is seen here as it is in Aries, however, with greater
tact and less bluntness which leads to a more prosperous
lifestyle.

Mercury in Scorpio is not beneficial when it concerns
health. In the 6th House, it may cause disorders of the intestinal
or generative systems.

When in 10° of Scorpio, health may be better and if the
luminaries are placed favourably, the native may live a long life.

In 20° of Scorpio the planet is harmful for the native's
status. Unfavourable company may mar his position. There is
serious threat of theft, fraud or even death when in the 8th
House.

Astro Advice

- Do not accept gifts from the blind.
- Donate copper.

Mercury in Sagittarius

Mercury situated in Sagittarius is highly beneficial for the growth of the native and he may prosper in the field of administration. He is equipped to be a government officer and if signified by the 3rd House, he may prosper in a diplomatic profession. The planet in this sign is also beneficial for foreign trade, exports, etc. Wealth will be earned with considerable effort since fortune shall not favour him.

In 10° of Sagittarius, the picture is better. The planet may bring prosperity provided the native uses wisdom. Profound thinking will be required before taking any decision. There exists the possibility of setbacks over issues related to the House occupied by this sign.

Mercury in 20° of Sagittarius results in the native being cautious, hesitant in thinking and wishing to keep what he has. However, to do that he should never stop being careful since the most minor deviation can result in his failure, if Mars, Saturn or Uranus throw adverse aspects.

Astro Advice

- Wear *Panna* of seven carats on the little finger on Wednesday morning.

Mercury in Capricorn

This is not a beneficial position. Old age and youth do not go together and if Saturn is not in good aspect with Mercury, it is definitely an indication of serious problems related to issues ruled by the House in which the sign sits. Aside from the Angular Houses, this situation is highly unfavourable for the native's health and may result in disorders of the nervous system. However, he is well equipped and has a keen mind for perusal of abstract topics. Since this is not conducive, the financial standing may not be very good.

When in 10° of Capricorn, the native may not do very well in legal business, however will progress in illegal ones. If the planet is well aspected by benefices, it signifies prosperity, however, retirement will be the native's way of life.

In 20° of Capricorn, the situation is better with reference to health issues and the native shall lead a long life. However it is not a favourable position for matrimony. This is the position of solitariness. One who lives away from relations, has few acquaintances who hardly bother about his well being.

Astro Advice

• Wear silver earrings for 40 days.

Mercury in Aquarius

Situated in Aquarius, the planet brings much enjoyment via friendship. The native's acquaintances will be educated and he shall like being amid them and vice-versa. Herein, Mercury also signifies loyalty and generosity. It is beneficial for alliances and even for mothers and offsprings.

When in 10° of Aquarius, the planet makes the native more diplomatic, a bit miserly but also adept. It is also beneficial for a fortune rich marriage which the native should look for, however, this will take place later in life and may be a cause for marital arguments.

In 20° of Aquarius, the planet is favourable for all mental matters and indicates an individual with aesthetic and cultured tastes. It indicates dealing in antique goods and this may result in the native's prosperity.

Astro Advice

- Give *Moong dal* to birds.
- Avoid bad company.

Mercury in Pisces

This situation signifies lack of loyalty in marriage or love, generally from the native's side. It also indicates rumours about the native which may harm him and his status, particularly in matters related to the heart.

In 10° of Pisces, Mercury gives the native many short-lived relationships. His acquaintances are as changeable as his thoughts and desires. When Mercury is in this decanate, life is not very fruitful.

In 20° of Pisces, the situation is much brighter. The native is honoured and will do well in foreign trade. The planet signifies intelligence that definitely brings prosperity.

Astro Advice

- Keep money plant in your bedroom.

Venus

This planet is beneficial, gainful, moist, negative, attractive and temperate. It is the planet representing love, relationships, pleasure, beauty, art. Its day domicile is in Libra and night in Taurus. Its exile is in Scorpio and Aries. This planet is often referred to as the Lesser Fortune.

Its metal is copper and day is Friday. In a layout of cards, it indicates woman, the female.

The planet makes the native gentle, generous, loving and happy with a liking for pleasure and comfort. Physically, he is gifted with fine features and is well formed. Venus makes the native somewhat self-centred since he wants pleasure for himself to be of topmost priority.

It results in ailments of the chest and the generative system mainly as a result of overindulgence.

VENUS IN THE HOUSES

Venus in the First House

Venus placed in the 1ˢᵗ House exercises a beneficial influence

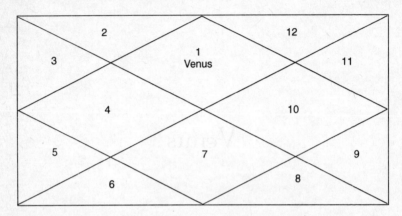

over the entire life of the native, unless afflicted, and bestows qualities such as a gentle and affectionate temperament, good manners and a love and appreciation of the aesthetic and artistic.

The native shall enjoy good health and will lead a long life unless Mars throws an adverse aspect, in which case it would cause severe illnesses resulting from overindulgence in pleasures and comforts.

With an adverse influence, this key in the First House brings many affairs of the heart, disloyalty and problems of the chest and spine.

Astro Advice

• Give grains to a white cow.

Venus in the Second House

This is a beneficial situation for business ventures, unless placed in a sign that is not favourable. The native shall

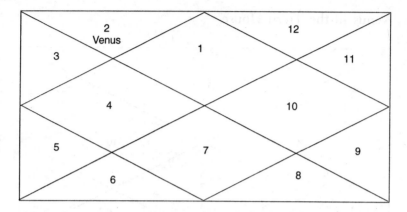

enter into a matrimonial alliance with a rich partner who will also keep him happy and he will prosper in all fields. The 2nd House being the House of personal worth, bestows definite aesthetic sense, and if the 3rd House is favourably situated, these artistic inclinations shall lead to fame and fortune.

This does give the native a tendency to splurge money on himself and others. He likes costly garments in pastel or light wear. He also has a desire to be of assistance to other people who are rich, happy, cultured and of a high status.

In a woman's chart this position is not that favourable for matrimony since the spouse is an incorrigible spender, flirt and gambler.

Astro Advice

- Offer sugar, rice, milk products at the place of worship on Friday before 11 in the morning.

Venus in the Third House

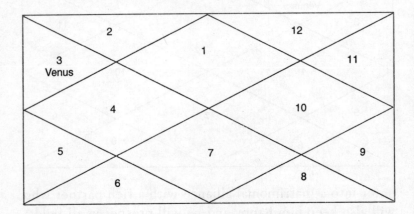

This position showers domestic accord and shows many pleasure trips. The native shall have refined education, unless there exist some adverse aspects.

He shall have a penchant for beauty and culture. This placing is for writers. This position makes the native prefer unknown people over family members. However, he shall always have cordial terms with them.

In the horoscope of a woman, the planet in the 3rd House signifies an encounter with a cultured man while on a trip. The alliance may not be monetarily gratifying, however, it shall be of high social status.

Astro Advice

- Your lucky jewels are diamond, topaz and high class light-coloured stones.

Venus in the Fourth House

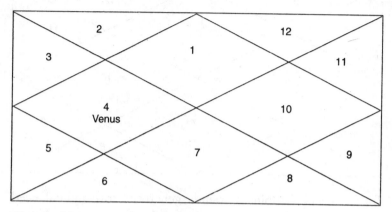

This enables the native to get continuous joy and peace in his home. His house shall also be done up in an exquisite style. There is also the definite indication that the native shall get money, property or inheritances from either his mother, wife or other women.

The native shall enjoy a carefree, happy and long life. If Mars or Saturn is on evil aspect with Venus in the nadir of the Heavens, it implies that the mother or wife may pass away early and unexpectedly.

Astro Advice

- Fondness of pets must be avoided.

Venus in the Fifth House

This is the true placing of the planet and herein it holds a strong influence over pleasure and feelings. It bestows a liking

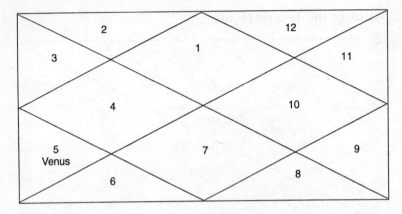

for socialising, happiness, friends, generosity, love and balanced thinking. It is fortunate for taking risks, betting, speculations and also, for a big family particularly of girls. However, this is possible, provided Saturn is not adversely aspected with Venus.

The planet, if dignified in the 5th House gets monetary prosperity in an artistic profession or it might make the native interested in things related to recreational places.

For females, this situation is an indication of early love intrigues. If influenced adversely or not well positioned, the planet may bring disillusionment in matters of the heart.

Astro Advice

• Must donate silver, milk, rice to a temple.

Venus in the Sixth House

In the 6th House the planet is not very significant with reference to health issues and is definitely not beneficial for the same, particularly for Pisces, Scorpio or Cancer.

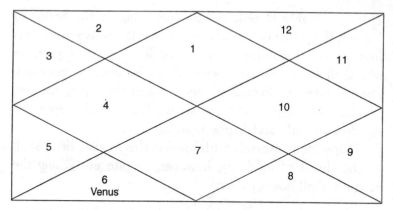

When dignified, it is good for home life which shall be happy and peaceful. It also signifies loyal and truthful workers. This position is favourable for uncles and aunts and might lead to a legacy from a relation.

Astro Advice

• Prayer to Sri Laxmi or Durga is advised.

Venus in the Seventh House

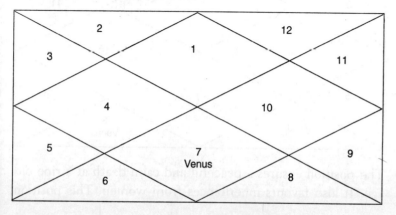

This is a highly beneficial situation being in the house of Unions, the planet being the ruler of love. It bestows numerous friends and acquaintances, wise and loyal business partners who shall add to the native's wealth. It also lets him enter into gainful alliances, succeed in business and therefore, ensures, that he will attain good social status. If dignified properly, it signifies an early and happy marriage.

If apsected adversely with Mars in this House, there shall be the threat of infidelity, however, despite everything the partners shall not separate.

Astro Advice

- Prayer to Mahalakshmi; *puja* to *panchmukha deepam* is beneficial.

Venus in the Eighth House

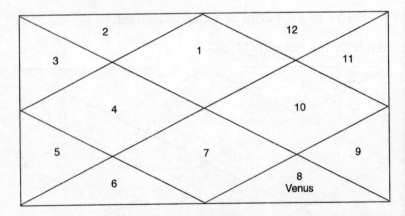

The position ensures a peaceful and calm death at a ripe old age. It also favours inheritances from women. This position also indicates a favourable marriage and prosperity in all spheres. An adverse aspect of Mars indicates the probability of loss of spouse. An aspect of Saturn shows the possibility of an alliance with a widow/widower.

Astro Advice

- Give full respect to your in-laws.

Venus in the Ninth House

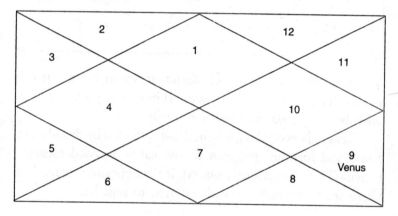

This situation is beneficial for mental matters and long trips. It signifies marriage with a foreigner and even if this does not happen, the alliance shall always be with a rich and intelligent person. The position bestows a liking for philosophy and theology, particularly in families.

Astro Advice

- Donate seven grains to a Brahmin lady.

Venus in the Tenth House

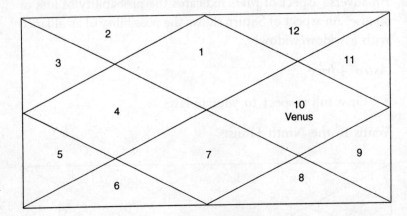

Venus in this House, if well dignified, ensures the native's prosperity in his chosen profession. It bestows a post of esteem with both material and social rewards.

Generally everything is beneficially affected by this placing. Fame and fortune are given to the native in good measure provided Venus is strongly placed. If the opposite is true, then there shall be problems with relation to females.

Astro Advice

• Immerse four square pieces of silver in flowing water.

Venus in the Eleventh House

The native shall be assisted by many powerful acquaintances. The planet in this House is also beneficial for offsprings who shall be strong and beautiful. It also endows the native with

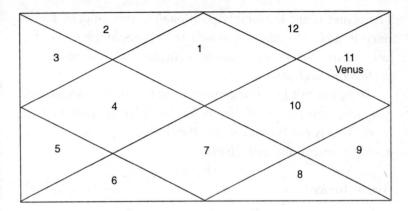

popularity and particularly with women who shall enable him to rise in society.

Astro Advice

• Donate silver at the place of worship.

Venus in the Twelfth House

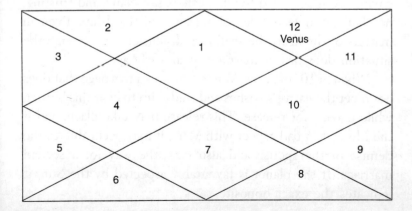

The planet is not favourably positioned in this unlucky house since it takes the native towards those people who are of a low status and it also indicates vague and dishonourable professions and affairs.

It may result in estrangement from the spouse because of rumours, particularly if Venus has an adverse aspect from Mars. This is not favourable for the health of the native since it causes infections and illnesses.

Astro Advice

• Donate sugar, rice, white cloth.

VENUS IN THE SIGNS

Venus in Aries

When placed in Aries, Venus does not bestow a fair amount of determination. It makes the native fickle and prone to paying too much heed to what others say. Naive and trusting, he shall often face a lot of tension and hardship. Even in matters of the heart, he shall face disillusionment though the situation does favour marriage at an early age.

When in 10° of Aries, Venus indicates a marriage that does not meet the native's wishes and leads him to bear this burden while craving for release. This release may take place, and if the Moon is in bad aspect with Mars, it may occur due to the demise of the spouse and also pave the way for a second marriage. If the planet is favourably aspected by the Sun, it indicates the exact opposite.

When in 20° of Aries, the planet leads to the estrangement of the partners since the tastes and ideas of the partner and the native are not in accordance with one another. This is more so in a female horoscope, in which case, it indicates an aggressive and crude husband, particularly if an adverse aspect is cast by Mars.

Astro Advice

- Avoid drinks and non-vegetarian food.

Venus in Taurus

When situated in its own domicile and aspected beneficially, the planet is favourable for matrimony since it achieves a balance between the heart and the mind. If adversely aspected then it signifies a changeable but gentle mate. The planet in conjunction or square with Mars in Taurus indicates problems in matters of the heart. Favourably aspected Venus is an indicator of prosperity in all matters. It is the Lesser Fortune and gets enjoyment in all the issues ruled by the House in which it is situated.

When in 10° of Taurus, Venus is a symbol of matrimonial infidelity. It indicates envy and an alteration of love and feelings.

When in 20° of Taurus, the planet is an indication of excessive ardour. The native adores one who does not reciprocate, as a result of which he feels tense. If Saturn afflicts with Venus if signifies many griefs. With an aspect at the Moon or Mercury, particularly in the 3rd House, it signifies a trip in connection with love but this may not get the desired result.

Astro Advice

- Offer water to the rising sun.

Venus in Gemini

When in this sign, the planet brings a number of acquaintances. The native is liked and loved by everyone. However he may not be as profoundly loving and this may hurt a few hearts. It is also a symbol of infidelity in marriage or that the native is the object of affection of two people at the same time. Venus in Gemini is also a sign that the offspring shall be beautiful and if the 5th House is beneficial and the Moon is favourably situated and aspected the native shall be blessed with twins.

When in 10° of Gemini, the planet is a symbol of indecisiveness and changeability in matters of the heart. Also, it indicates worry due to the beloved and also envy.

When in 20° of Gemini, the planet and situation is much better. It indicates the chance of prosperity and progress in issues ruled by the house in which Venus is situated. It signifies amicability, loyalty and fame.

Astro Advice

- Get up early in the morning and touch the earth with the right hand.

Venus in Cancer

Venus situated in Cancer is not a favourable position. It signifies unfaithfulness, changeability and secret liaisons. An adverse aspect of Mars brings about estrangement from the spouse. It might be an indication of entering into matrimony with either a divorcee or a widow/widower. It does not favour accord in marriage and is the reason for arguments particularly if the Moon is in evil aspect and if the planet is in the 4th House. If the planet is favourably aspected, it indicates prosperity but no emotional richness. Venus, strictly speaking, may not bring sadness in affairs of the heart but it does make the native get easily bored which is why he causes greater grief to others than to himself.

When in 10° of Cancer, Venus indicates in all certainty estrangement from the spouse. It also signifies threat of mishaps or injuries due to reasons related to love, particularly if Mars emanates an adverse aspect to Venus.

When in 20° of Cancer, it gives the native the ability to conquer difficulties in love and be happy despite everything, even if it means taking an aggressive stand which is beneficial in some alliances, especially if the mate is strongly influenced by Venus.

Astro Advice

• Give eatables to birds.

Venus in Leo

The planet situated in this sign is beneficial for an early marriage, unless it is affected by adverse aspects. The alliance shall get happiness, respect and contentment for the native. This is true even with adverse aspects. However, in that case the alliance is short lived. Boredom and tiredness will soon set in. The native or his mate are oblivious of what life is all about and wish to know it better (particularly in 20° of Leo). This will therefore, result in many irritations and arguments which shall be hard to resolve.

When in 10° of Leo, the planet symbolises loyalty and the matrimonial alliance shall cease only with the demise of the one of the mates. However if Mars sends out an adverse aspect, there shall be fights but these shall not last for long since the partners will be bound by immense physical attraction.

Astro Advice

- Immerse oil in flowing water.

Venus in Virgo

Venus placed in Virgo is not beneficial for marriage. It brings strange notions about love which is more physical than emotional. An adverse aspect of Mars, Saturn or the Moon may signify sexual perversity.

This placement creates single people – nuns, monks, spinsters and bachelors. If Saturn aspects Venus, it may result in sex disorders.

When in 20° of Virgo the planet is not beneficial for matters of the heart. It frequently signifies an alliance with a rich but much older person and this causes trouble to the native later since Venus, herein, signifies moral isolation.

Astro Advice

• Worship any goddess.

Venus in Libra

When situated in her most beneficial domicile, Venus bestows a character of a high order, one that has a taste for the finer things of life. It is the perfect situation for artists and sophisticated people. The native will enter into a financially and socially enriching marriage which shall bring joy unless the Sun is in conjunction with Venus, in which case it indicates estrangement very soon. As it happens with many marriages, this shall not take place without resulting in a lot of envy and hatred from people around the partners. However with a favourable aspect they shall remain satisfied and happy.

When in 10° of Libra, this situation is highly fortunate for a man. It shall enable him to ascend great heights by virtue of his own luck and intellect. Herein, the planet lets the native take risks and do anything since he is led by love and achieves prosperity.

When in 20° of Libra, the planet signifies plenty and steadiness. However, an adverse aspect of Mars on Venus shall bring tension with reference to offsprings particularly if this takes place in the 5th or 11th House.

Astro Advice

• All family members should offer food to cows.

Venus in Scorpio

Venus's situation in Scorpio (one of Mars's domicile) is not beneficial. It results in numerous problems and difficulties with reference to issues ruled by the house. In the 5th House, it might bring about the demise of an offspring. In the 6th House, it indicates ailments of the generative system, in the 8th House, it signifies the early death of the wife. When situated in a female's horoscope, it indicates serious disillusionment in matters related to love and emotions and is frequently indicative of the deception and loss of trust in a girl's life. If Venus is aspected by the Moon in the 4th House, it signifies a child born out of wedlock.

When in 10° Scorpio, the planet signifies arguments between the marriage partners, estrangement and a second marriage which will probably be as bad as the first one. When in a man's horoscope, it signifies that he shall be involved in many affairs and shall cheat women, and if Mars aspects Venus, it signifies that he will have a mishap of some sort.

When in 20° of Scorpio, it indicates unfaithfulness, arguments and unpleasantness in marriage. When in the 7th House, it brings about dishonour, estrangement, court cases and the threat of being cheated by the spouse. However, if the aspect takes place in the 1st House then the native may try to cheat the society.

Astro Advice

- Donate seven kg rice to the place of worship.

Venus in Sagittarius

Venus placed in Sagittarius is highly beneficial for eminent artists upon whom it shall shower wealth, fame and honour. However, it is not beneficial for matrimony. Marriage is delayed and may take place even if there is no love involved and if adversely aspected by Mars, it shall bring disrepute.

When in 10° of Sagittarius, the planet results in profound love being more important for the native rather than passion and this will be enriching both from the financial and emotional point of view, provided Venus is not afflicted.

When in 20° of Sagittarius, Venus signifies a matrimonial alliance of convenience rather than love. Venus if aspected by Mars and in the 8th House signifies widowhood.

Astro Advice

• Give food to a blind beggar.

Venus in Capricorn

When situated in Capricorn, Venus is not beneficial for either love or matrimony. It makes the native highly changeable and strange in matters of the heart. If the planet is favourably aspected, particularly in the 7th House, the native shall be married to an older person of a Saturnian temperament and the home shall be sad and devoid of children. If Mars casts an adverse aspect and Venus is in the 5th House, then the offspring shall pass away at an early age. Venus in Capricorn also brings about arguments between the marital partners.

When in 10° of Capricorn, the planet brings peril with reference to women. An adverse aspect of Saturn may result in death because of sadness, particularly in a woman's horoscope, or, if indicated by the chart. On the whole death may occur as a result of suicide with Mars, Venus and Saturn in square aspect and Venus being placed in the decanate in the 8th House. When in 20° of Capricorn, the situation is much better. The problems related to love stay, however, desolation remains but there is no threat of death since the determination of the native bounces back even after disillusionment in matters regarding affections.

Astro Advice

• Give full respect to your elders.

Venus in Aquarius

Venus situated in Aquarius is not beneficial for the native's struggle in life since it bestows a feminine and lazy temperament, too much generosity or even fragility. If the horoscope is lucky, the placement of Venus shall be favourable and signifies that the native shall have a stable, happy life. If the sign is placed in the 4th House, the domestic scenario will be peaceful, calm, somewhat filled with accord and this is what the native wants.

But if the horoscope depicts hardships, then Venus is not beneficial since it shall result in the estrangement of the married partners due to the native's feebleness. Unfaithfulness and secret liaisons may take place which may result in the loss or gain of money depending upon how Mercury is positioned and aspected.

When in 10° of Aquarius, the planet is unfavourably placed with reference to love. It signifies cheating and deceit but this shall favour the native financially to some extent.

When in 20° of Aquarius, the situation is more favourable and will bring favours and gains that shall be more enduring in nature and will be brought about by the assistance of an individual of the opposite gender.

Astro Advice

•   Keep distance from bad company.

Venus in Pisces

Positioned in Pisces the planet signifies that the native shall marry early and also, there will be two marriages. For a man, if the sign is situated in the 8th House, it indicates that he will lose his wife to death early in life while for a woman it implies that she will have a much older man as her spouse and he will pamper her thoroughly. Financially, the situation is favourable since Venus in Jupiter's domicile is devoid of any affliction and showers good fortune, thereby allowing the native to prosper in all his ventures, particularly in an angular house.

When placed in 10° of Pisces, the planet loses a few of its good qualities since it indicates arguments caused by lies and cheating in love affairs. It brings about unfaithfulness and estrangement. It may also result in the loss of status if Venus is afflicted by Uranus, in which case ill-luck will be related with the particular house.

In 20° of Pisces, the planet showers immense joy at home. It brings accord between partners, healthy offspring and a comfortable financial status. However, all this depends upon the fact that there are no adverse aspects.

Astro Advice

• Wear diamond on your ring finger.

Jupiter

A fortunate and beneficial planet, Jupiter signifies protection. It is referred to as the Greater Fortune and it makes the favourable aspects in a horoscope stronger and reduces the unfavourable ones.

The planet is dry, temperate and beneficial, its metal is copper, colour pale or purple-blue and day is Thursday.

Jupiter's day domicile is in Sagittarius, night is in Pisces. Its exaltation is in Cancer and its fall is in Capricorn. Its Joy is in Sagittarius and it is in exile in Gemini and Virgo.

It is nearest to earth when in Aries and farthest when in Libra.

It creates officials of the government, church and foreign relations. It exerts special effect on businessmen and all those who hold special posts.

It endows the native with a happy, generous and pleasant temperament. It also makes the native fond of pomp and show and social gatherings. He is also very fond of his family, is highly methodical and values honour and status. However, he does have the tendency to boast and be proud.

The planet signifies a native who is reasonably tall, strong, oval-faced with a high forehead. The native is inclined to premature baldness and sweating. It gives a tendency for excessive adipose tissue at a young age. The planet is a friend of the Moon and an enemy of Mars.

It confers a tendency for ailments such as gout and apoplexy.

JUPITER IN THE HOUSES

Jupiter in the First House

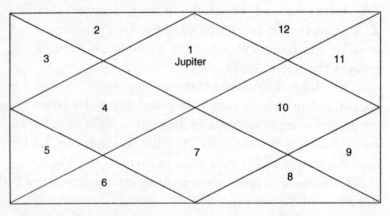

When situated in the 1st House, the planet brings good opportunities for rising higher in life in keeping with the social atmosphere that surrounds the native. It also endows an aspiring nature and the wish to grow in truthful and legal ways.

If there are no adverse aspects from Mars, the native shall have a long life with a great deal of good fortune, honours and influential acquaintances.

Astro Advice

• Pour water on the Tulsi plant.

Jupiter in the Second House

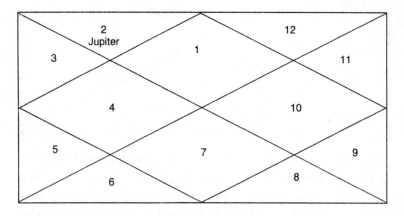

The placing of Jupiter in the 2nd House is indeed a fortunate one since it bestows definite profits in an occupation ruled by Jupiter, such as a large business. It is also beneficial for acquiring property or wealth.

When the situation takes place in a favourable sign, it assures a financially promising marriage in a good family. However, such a situation may rob the native of love in his childhood, or accord in the family since the parents may be divorced or estranged, particularly if the planet is in a fire sign.

Astro Advice

• Give food to five Brahmins.

Jupiter in the Third House

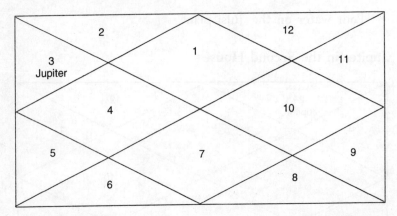

When situated in the 3rd House, the planet is beneficial for academics and issues linked with the intellect. It often indicates that the native has been raised in a spiritual fashion. This situation is of those who hold many degrees and certificates. It also bestows amicable relations between parents, siblings and acquaintances. Since this house rules over travelling, the planet indicates the same, and journeys shall be undertaken in comfort. It also indicates the opportunity of entering into a business alliance with one's parents, and provided that there are no adverse aspects of Mars, this will be very lucky.

Depending upon the aptitude of the native, the planet will make him the agent of an important business or government enterprise.

Astro Advice

• Fast on *Ekadashi*.

Jupiter in the Fourth House

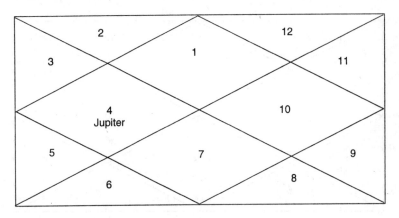

Situated in the 4th House, Jupiter signifies an esteemed lineage. It also indicates good health and immunity from illness. It bestows a fondness for the home and hearth, a liking for comfort and indicates an organised and orderly temperament.

It indicates profits through property and signifies financial protection from the father. If the Sun is placed well, it signifies inherited and increased fortune.

This situation assures fame and influence towards the end of life provided that the 10th House is influential.

Also the native's life shall be quite long and favourable particularly from the age of 40.

Astro Advice

• Avoid conjugal activities in daylight.

Jupiter in the Fifth House

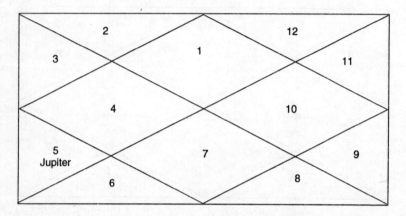

When situated in this House, the planet endows the native with many beautiful children who shall bring a great deal of joy. This situation may make the native highly changeable, particularly if Mars and Venus have an adverse aspect in the horoscope. There is a dominance of a fondness for gambling, merry making and recreation. It denotes the idea of a bank manager or theatre/media person.

Jupiter, when dignified and in the 5th House, gets success, status and prestige. The individual enjoys a life of comfort and good luck.

The native is quite self-centred. However, he may also be generous and helpful at times. The planet in this House helps achieve one's goal. If Mars emits a wicked aspect or is not strong and is ruler of the first house, the individual shall witness a slight decline in status but will increase his wealth.

When placed in this House, the planet brings about chances of a financially beneficial matrimonial alliance.

Astro Advice

• Seek the blessings of elders in the morning.

Jupiter in the Sixth House

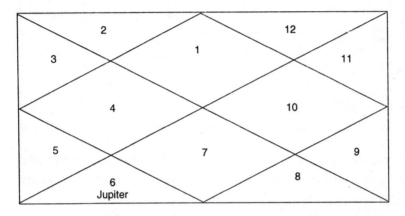

Jupiter, if dignified, brings favourable health. However there may be some minor digestive and circulatory ailments in the fiftieth year.

As far as social status is concerned the planet is not very beneficial. It indicates a junior post with an average income and a sedate life style.

Astro Advice

• Your lucky jewel is high class transparent ruby and *pukhraj*.

Jupiter in the Seventh House

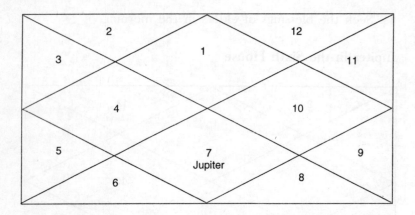

When situated in the 7th House, the planet is extremely beneficial for business alliances as well as for all other kinds of unions.

The situation indicates loss of spouse and if the planet is in Gemini, Virgo or Pisces, then the possibility of a second marriage exists.

The position endows the native with a good social life, victory over adversaries and peace in old age. However, there exists a lack of love particularly if it is in Sagittarius.

If adversely aspected, the planet brings many problems, particularly with matters related to the heart.

Astro Advice

• You must make maximum use of gold on your body.

Jupiter in the Eighth House

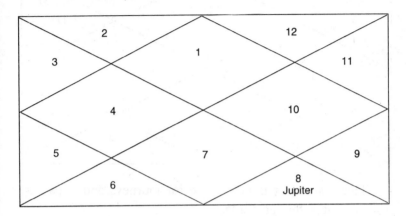

Placed in the 8th House, Jupiter if beneficially aspected in Sagittarius, Pisces or Cancer brings wealth through legacies or matrimony. The planet in this House and in Capricorn is not at all beneficial; it indicates financial difficulties and sickness which may be fatal.

If dignified, the planet gives the native the certainty of a natural and calm death.

Astro Advice

• Maintenance of silence (*Mauna Vrata*) brings good results.

Jupiter in the Ninth House

When situated in the 9th House the planet has a favourable influence on the morality and intelligence of the native. It endows him with wisdom, balance, peace and high ideals. He well immerse himself in theology or spiritualism.

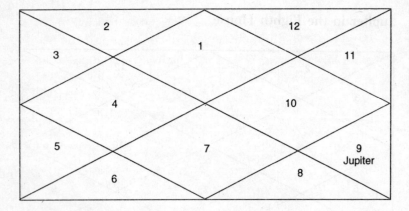

This placement is favourable for journeys and trips and also indicates foreign trade.

Astro Advice

- Offer milk, *laddu*, sugar, rice, *ghee* to Brahmins on Thursdays.

Jupiter in the Tenth House

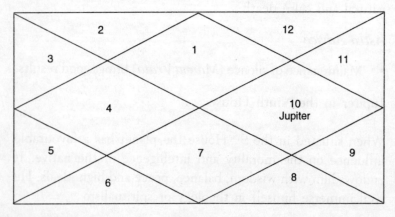

This placement is the most beneficial position in a horoscope as far as social status and prestige are concerned. If the planet is favourably aspected, it signifies a high and esteemed position. It is a definite indication of riches and joy.

Astro Advice

• The north-east is a favourable direction.

Jupiter in the Eleventh House

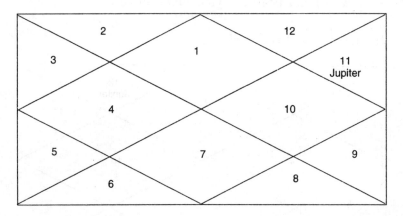

In the 11th House, Jupiter is beneficial for issues related to politics since it makes the native a leader whom many people will follow. His friend circle is congenial and since he is fond of socialising there will be a great deal of drinking, dancing and dining.

The native's helpfulness, good humour and intelligence shall win him popularity, success and help realise his aspirations.

He shall get married at an early age and have many children who shall be a source of joy. If the Moon is favourably aspected, then in a male horoscope, it signifies sons while in a female horoscope, it signifies daughters.

Also in a woman's horoscope, this position is favourable for marriage and the alliance will give birth to someone who will hold a high position.

Astro Advice

- *Pukhraj* and pearl are your lucky stones.

Jupiter in the Twelfth House

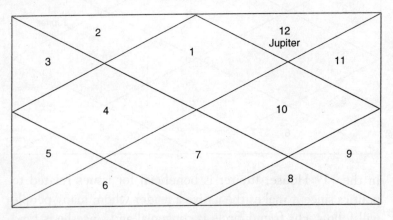

In the 12th House, the planet bestows assistance and protection enabling the native to shield himself from hardships and make friends of enemies.

The individual is gentle, benevolent and enjoys making other people happy.

If situated in an unlucky sign, it is not good for marriage. If adversely influenced by Saturn, it indicates decline in social status. Mars however, alters the opinion held by others about the native.

Astro Advice

- Recite the following *mantra* 108 times in the morning after bath:
  'Aum Hran Hrin Hron Bren Brihaspate Namah'.

JUPITER IN THE SIGNS

Jupiter in Aries

The planet situated in Aries bestows the individual with a lot of ambition and determination. It makes him a dominating, yet impartial and gentle leader. With favourable aspects, it enables the native to reach great heights by virtue of his own capabilities.

When in 10° of Aries, the planet indicates a late but fulfilling marriage, particularly for a woman.

When in 20° of Aries, it gives the native the strength to face problems, avoid traps and hold on to his faith and belief. His immunity to sickness is good and though he may fall ill he shall recover very soon.

Astro Advice

- Give yellow cloth to a poor man.

Jupiter in Taurus

Situated in Taurus, the planet indicates a financially favourable matrimonial alliance. Both marriage partners will ensure that their domestic life is harmonious and happy.

In a male horoscope, the native earns the admiration of women and is an adept lover. However, if adversely aspected by Mars in 10° of Taurus all this will be reversed and there shall be a great deal of envy, disputes and differences. It also indicates unfaithfulness and domestic discord.

When in 20° of Taurus, the planet is an indicator of problems in climbing up the social ladder. It also signifies that from the age of 30 the native will hold a high post which will take him on a journey and also prevent him from settling down into domestic life for quite some time.

Astro Advice

• Worship womanhood or any goddess.

Jupiter in Gemini

Jupiter is in exile in Gemini and is not beneficial for the emotional state of the native. The native places more emphasis on financial gains and materialism and hence loses out on the happiness and contentment that love and affection bring. Though he shall achieve a good position till the age of 45, he will be unhappy due to disappointment in matters relating to feelings and emotions. He may or may not have a family, depending upon the position of Venus and Moon in Jupiter which are quite adversely placed in 20° of Gemini.

When in 10° of Gemini, Jupiter makes the native the top boss in business. It bestows him with an inclination for numbers and an organised mind which will enable him to progress.

This situation does make the native very rich and famous, however, once again, it is not beneficial for matrimony.

Astro Advice

• Avoid alcohol and intoxication.

Jupiter in Cancer

Situated in Cancer, the planet bestows good fortune on the native. It brings unforeseen profit and allows him to earn money through gambling. Prosperity comes by virtue of good fortune rather than the native's own hard work. His status will be established both in his own land and overseas.

When in 10° of Cancer, the planet is in the sign of its exaltation and as a result is responsible for journeys and travel.

When in 20° of Cancer, the situation is just as favourable. Though good fortune remains, the native also has to work himself in order to prosper and this will be good for him.

Astro Advice

• Pour black wine in flowing water.

Jupiter in Leo

When placed in Leo, Jupiter endows the native with lofty ideals, intelligence and generosity. Fortune smiles on him and whatever he takes up will be completed in a fulfilling manner as long as Mars and Saturn do not disrupt this balance.

When in 10° of Leo, the planet brings a vast social circle which shall enable the native to prosper yet make him vulnerable to rumour and gossip. He should not reveal his plans to one and all.

When in 20° of Leo, the planet enables the native to conquer hardship and difficulties which may arise due to his esteemed post.

Jupiter in Leo in the 6th House may cause blood or heart ailments if adversely influenced by Mars.

Astro Advice

• Get up before sunrise.

Jupiter in Virgo

Situated in Virgo, the planet does not bring status for the native, however, it makes him gentle, careful, clever and somewhat proud. It indicates many romantic entanglements but most of them are transient. The native is self-reliant and hardworking and prospers through his own merit.

When in 10° of Virgo, there may be some problems with reference to social status at the age of 45. Though it indicates a hard life, the native faces it happily and gives the impression of a fortunate man.

When in 20° of Virgo, the planet is very fortunate for love and marriage. It is beneficial for the native to marry the daughter of his boss since it will enable him to prosper financially.

Astro Advice

- Fast on Thursdays.

Jupiter in Libra

This is a placement which affects issues relating to law, art, politics and medicine with favourable aspects. The planet is good in all the spheres. The 30th and 40th years indicate significant stages of social success. It also signifies many companions who shall be of great assistance.

When in 10° of Libra, the native has the ability to understand and be understood under the influence of Jupiter. The planet bestows logic and intellect, an inclination for art and form. Thus, this position makes great lawyers, professors or artists. If adversely aspected by the Sun in the 7th House, then this position brings sadness in marriage and even estrangement.

When in 20° of Libra, it signifies an increase in status from the age of 40. From this time prosperity will be rapid and wealth and prestige shall be earned at the same time. As a result the native should be careful with finances towards his 50th year, if Mars sends an adverse aspect to Jupiter. Therefore, the native should invest his money carefully.

Astro Advice

- Give *gur* to five blind people.

Jupiter in Scorpio

The planet in Scorpio makes the native dominating and quarrelsome. He tends to subdue and suppress those around him and is able to do so through cunning. If Jupiter is favourably aspected he gets prosperity at a rapid pace.

When in 10° of Scorpio, the planet bestows the native with the best of health, strength and endurance. It may cause (particularly in Angular House) a decline in wealth and the native may have to start from the very beginning.

When in 20° of Scorpio, Jupiter causes problems through the wife or mother in a male horoscope and in a female horoscope through the father or husband.

This situation protects the native from cunning and cheating since the native is capable and intelligent.

Astro Advice

• Give yellow cloth to a Brahmin.

Jupiter in Sagittarius

When situated in Sagittarius, which is one of Jupiter's domiciles, the planet bestows a liking for athletics, hunting, horse-riding. The native enjoys a comfortable life and likes rural living. It is beneficial for occupations like farming and cattle rearing. He shall have a long and peaceful life, though old age may be lonely as a result of loss of the spouse.

When in 10° of Sagittarius, the planet brings prosperity, however, by virtue of physical work problems may crop up, yet if Jupiter is not adversely aspected by Saturn, prosperity will be accomplished by the age of 38.

When in 20° of Sagittarius, Jupiter gives the native the ability to know what he wants and how to achieve it. Progress may be slow but is assured.

Astro Advice

• Offer yellow pumpkin at the place of worship.

Jupiter in Capricorn

In Capricorn, Jupiter is not placed favourably. It signifies foes and opponents who do not allow the native to behave in a strong manner. The genes are not good and indicate fragility in offspring. The level of aspirations is low and life is dull and uninteresting.

When in 10° of Capricorn, the effect is unfavourable. However, the level of energy is high and prosperity may be achieved as a result of a favourable influence from the Moon.

When in 20° of Capricorn, both genes and health are better. However, the native is threatened towards the age of 43 by either a mishap or some sickness which will affect the circulatory system.

Astro Advice

• Seek the blessings of your parents daily.

Jupiter in Aquarius

Situated in Aquarius, the planet bestows the native with an inclination for the sciences. He is gifted with a logical mind and enjoys a peaceful, calm and secluded life. It is favourable for opportunities as inventors, mechanical engineers or lab scientists. The native does not have a liking for money and wealth and depending upon the aspect of Mars, the native will be either quarrelsome or peace-loving.

It indicates the chances of marriage with a person older than the native and this will be quite successful. If there are any arguments it will be the result of the native's laziness and lethargy.

When in 20° of Aquarius, it provides protection and the native's idealistic character takes him to a post of repute depending upon the aspects of the 3rd and 9th Houses.

Astro Advice

• Give foodgrains to crows.

Jupiter in Pisces

Jupiter in Pisces signifies that the native shall prosper by virtue of his own merit. He shall have the aid and assistance of his friends. However, this may disrupt his family life, particularly in 10° of Pisces, since competition may occur with a senior person. An adverse aspect of Mars in Jupiter signifies two marriages, probably the result of the early death of the spouse.

When in 20° of Pisces, the planet is responsible for a favourable post but under the employment of someone. If the decanate is in a favourable house, then the native's life will be long, happy, fulfilling and comfortable.

Astro Advice

* Get up early in the morning and offer water to the rising sun.

Mars

The planet is arid, hot and male. It is in exile in the domiciles of Venus (Libra and Taurus). Its day domicile is in Aries and night domicile in Scorpio. Its exaltation is in Capricorn and its fall is in Cancer. It receives joy in Scorpio.

When placed in Virgo it is the farthest from Earth and is the nearest when situated in Pisces.

Mars endows intensity, energy, growth and impetuosity alongwith an alert, active disposition.

In the lay out of cards Mars signifies life, vigour and anger. It symbolises the male and bestows bluntness.

The planet gives a sturdy constitution, average height and strong muscles. The ability to resist diseases and infection is great. Hair is generally brown with a slight reddish hue in it and is dry and rough. The face on the whole has an aura of strength and this is visible in the body as well. The overall manner is bold and authoritative.

Mars represents a man who will be attractive to females because of his robust, sturdy disposition. However, he may not generally vibe well with other men as with them he will often enter into disputes being vengeful. When influenced beneficially, the native shall have an exemplary temperament and will take up the cause of the helpless and frail, even if they are not right.

The planet bestows a liking for sports. When aspected with Mercury, it makes a pilot. It forms an excellent soldier in periods of war and gives a stable head in peace time.

Its metal is iron, day is Tuesday and colour is red. Its illnesses are fevers, inflammatory ailments and mishaps and injuries.

MARS IN THE HOUSES

Mars in the First House

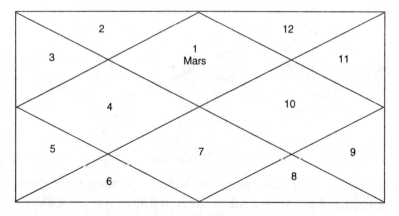

When Mars is placed in the 1st House, it signifies a tendency to exert power and influence over other people. It also symbolises physical and moral bravery, if the planet is aspected well; otherwise it might signify weakness and cause the native to hurt those who are weaker than his own self. It is quite frequently a symbol of arguments and fights. In a lay out of cards, if the planet comes out near the Ascendant, it surely signifies an emotional or intense event. Mars in the 1st House endows vigour, enthusiasm and spending of the life force of an individual.

Astro Advice

- Immerse sweets (like *gur*, sugar) in flowing water.

Mars in the Second House

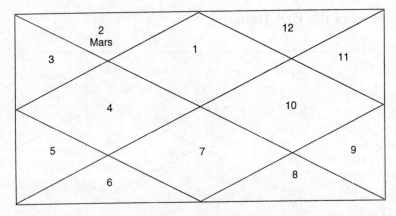

Mars in this House gives the native a tendency to spend lavishly. His desires shall be great and therefore, in order to maintain harmony, it will be necessary that he have a good amount of money. He shall also earn wealth by virtue of his own efforts. If Mars is well aspected the native will entertain a good number of strong ideas which shall not let him view things in a restricted perspective. His level of activity shall be high, however confusing. There may be disorganisation but this shall be made up for by an innate tendency for order and a good memory. Also, the planet in this House forms a leader and his juniors shall be affected by Jupiter or Mercury which shall negate the errors of their leader. This is a favourable situation when the planet is aspected well and positioned in one of his own signs. If Jupiter sends out a favourable aspect to this House, the native shall be married to a rich person and though this alliance may suffer from emotional poverty, financially it will be very gratifying.

However, if the planet is adversely placed in the 2nd House with bad aspects from Saturn or Uranus, there shall be a great deal of difficulties and monetary problems.

Astro Advice

•   You should offer *gur* or wheat in a place of worship.

Mars in the Third House

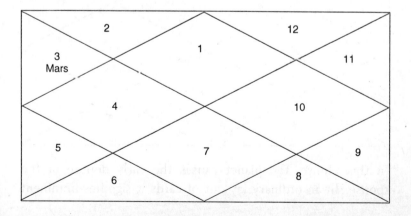

When placed in the 3rd House Mars shall be the causative factor for disputes with people around the native and also, the threat of physical injuries. There shall hardly be any accord between siblings as the native shall be childish and domineering. There also exist the chances of the parents being of a similar temperament. Since the native shall have the intellect of a critic, with good education he may become a high class political leader. This is not a beneficial situation from the point of view of travelling since mishaps are indicated mainly due to the native's carelessness.

Astro Advice

- *Tula-daan* of *desi-ghee*, wheat, orange, wine, copper can bring marvellous results.

Mars in the Fourth House

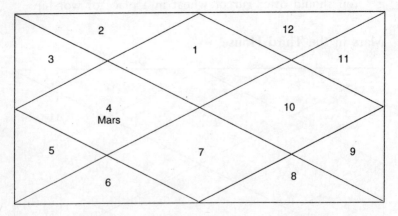

In this House, the planet causes the early demise of the spouse. In an ordinary lay out of cards it signifies imminent danger. In a horoscope, it symbolises circulatory ailments and the presence of a tyrannical person who shall mar domestic happiness. Moreover, such a situation also signifies ruin of property in a fire, particularly if the Sun is in a bad aspect with the planet. In the nadir of Heavens, Mars indicates the unexpected demise of the father as a result of a cardiac arrest or a mishap. If favourably aspected, the planet might cause an increase in profits by virtue of efforts. However, if it is not so, then there shall be perpetual problems.

Astro Advice

• Prayer to Rama, Hanuman will bring strong determination and goodwill.

Mars in the Fifth House

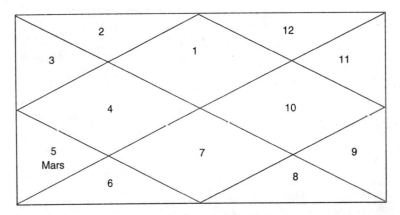

Mars in the 5th House signifies a disorderly and disorganised existence. The native leads a hard, poverty-stricken life and may be an unlucky gambler who will blow his money away.

This indicates mere pursuit of pleasurable activities with no regard for serious issues. An offspring may suffer from ailments peculiar to the sign in which the planet sits. As far as women are concerned, if the planet is badly aspected, there exists the chances of difficult childbirth and if these evil aspects come from Neptune, there lies the threat of a miscarriage. If the planet is dignified, offsprings shall be active, energetic and difficult to handle. They may also be aloof and self-reliant, however, success and prosperity will be theirs.

Astro Advice

- Recite the following *mantra* 108 times in the evening: *'Aum Kran Krin Kron Sae Angarkaye Namah.'*

Mars in the Sixth House

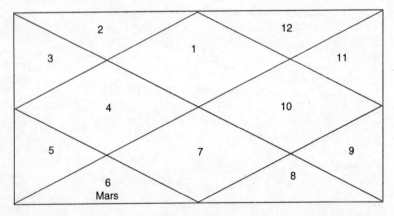

If the planet in this House is well aspected it signifies a good amount of immunity which shall enable the native to resist illness. However, if it is adversely aspected and placed in a negative sign, it shall cause fevers and inflammatory disorders in the body part which is ruled by that particular sign.

This situation leads to monetary gain and betterment of home environment. If adversely aspected it results in many arguments with workers.

The planet in this House symbolises violent theft by someone working in the house.

When placed in Scorpio in the 5th House, the planet affects those equipped to tend to their fellow beings.

Astro Advice

• Keep one red hakik stone in your purse.

Mars in the Seventh House

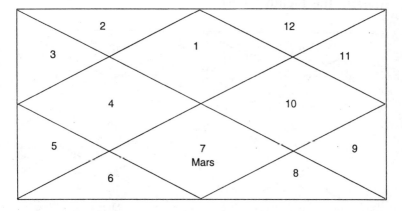

Mars in the 7th House bestows a large amount of passion and ardour, thereby, leading to an early affair or matrimony. If aspected favourably, it will result in a rich alliance with a woman who shall wish to dominate the household and shall have both good and bad points of the material type. If not well aspected, the partners shall not remain together particularly if the ascendant has a female planet since this causes irritation in the domestic scene due to the laziness of one partner and hyperactivity of the other. It also signifies loss of the spouse and is unfavourable for mergers and contracts.

When placed favourably and receiving beneficial aspects from Mercury, the planet in the 7th House is a definite sign that big steps shall be taken by the native and these shall bring profits as well as envy and court cases.

Astro Advice

- Donate sweets to the poor.

Mars in the Eighth House

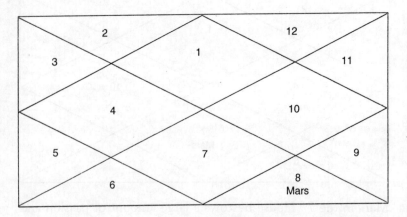

Mars placed in this House signifies the demise of the native or if aspected with the Sun or the Moon, the demise of either of the parents. If favourably aspected the native shall profit by this. If aspected with Venus it is a sign of unexpected death of the spouse who shall be of a violent and dominating temperament.

In a horoscope wherein Uranus, Moon or Saturn are affected this position indicates the probability of suicide.

Astro Advice

• Donate *Masoor dal* or immerse it in water.

Mars in the Ninth House

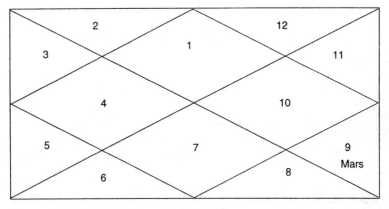

If dignified, Mars in this House indicates possibility of success for the native since it gives him mental and physical energy and initiative.

The native is blessed with an intelligent mind which helps him to view things in a broader perspective. Though the position indicates hardships, it may lead to success, provided that the sign occupied by Mars in the 9th House is influential and strong. However, if it is the opposite and if the planet is affected, it leads to depression, hesitation and arguments with parents.

The planet in this house leads to an inclination for journeys and travelling.

Astro Advice

• Immerse 11 coconuts in flowing water for 11 consecutive Tuesdays.

Mars in the Tenth House

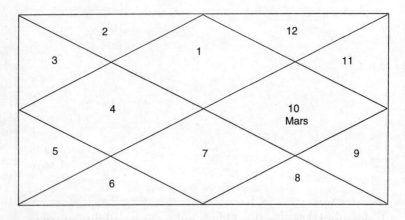

If dignified, the influence of Mars in mid-Heaven is indeed great. It benefits the most risky ventures and these can be completed successfully. This is the position of a politician or authoritarian chief, one who defeats his adversaries and avoids all traps. Though there may be hard times and a good deal of struggle, the native shall protect himself and if the horoscope is good, will learn to influence and dominate through struggle.

This is not a good position for a junior post. The native does not make a good employee unless given a great deal of freedom. When the planet is dignified in this House, it indicates success with females but arguments with the mother.

If Saturn is situated in the 4th House, it is a sign that the father may die an early death. It also signifies the native's own sudden demise. The planet in this house is a sure sign that the native will be violent and obstinate.

If Mar's position and aspects are not good in the 10th House, there may be devastating tragedies.

Astro Advice

- Recite Hanuman Chalisa on Tuesday evening in a temple 21 times.

Mars in the Eleventh House

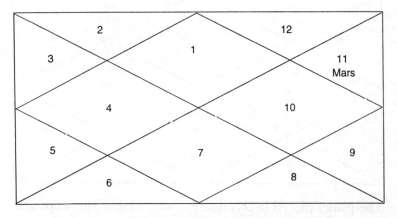

This is a negative situation and signifies many arguments and fights with friends or known people. It implies disputes between parents and offspring and shall result in their loss if Saturn is in the 5th House and gives a negative aspect.

If the planet is dignified in this house, it bestows influence and shall make a leader who will be less loved and held more in fear. However, for this to take place, the Sun, Jupiter or Venus must be in a favourable aspect.

Mars is the planet of achievements and aims and it shall achieve its goals but may cause grief to some people.

Astro Advice

- Recite the *Mantra* 108 times in the evening:
  'Aum Aan Angarkaye Namah'.

Mars in the Twelfth House

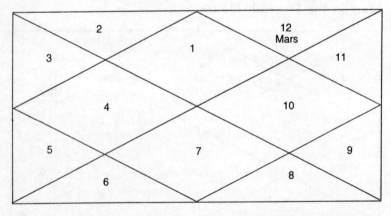

The planet placed in this house causes a lot of hardships and struggle because of a display of naivete bordering on idiocy. If Venus is afflicted in the 7th House, there shall be infidelity.

If Mercury is in the 7th House, it indicates problems with the law and also, imprisonment. If the Moon is afflicted in the 9th House, the native may suffer from madness. Mars in the 12th House cannot be lucky considering that the minimum damage it can do is through operations or mishaps.

Favourable aspects from Jupiter, Venus or the Sun may source the problems, which may be many and perpetual and which the native shall regard as the spice of his life.

Astro Advice

• Donate *gur* every Tuesday at a religious place.

MARS IN THE SIGNS

Mars in Aries

When situated in its own domicile, the planet is quite powerful, especially over emotions and feelings rather than the mind and intellect.

Such a situation endows the native with self-reliance, obstinacy, skillfulness and recklessness. It may even make him angry and rash and could lead to mishaps and head injuries following some disputes.

With a beneficial influence from Mercury or Saturn, the planet signifies mind games or work in the charge of a professional or intelligent man.

In 10° of Aries, the planet bestows a wish to serve, however also a tendency to interfere with the lives of others, to don the mantle of a feeble person and therefore, get involved in problems.

This situation gives the native the capability of taking up seemingly difficult tasks and completing them successfully.

In 20° of Aries, an adverse aspect from Saturn indicates the threat of a mishap or of serious ill-luck in issues dominated by the House.

Astro Advice

- Donate *channa dal*, *gur*, *ghee*, and red cloth.

Mars in Taurus

When Mars is situated in Taurus, it signifies an intense, emotional and frequently sensuous disposition, however, somewhat inconstant. This situation is not safe for a female as it results in extreme emotional turbulence particularly when the planet is in the 7th House.

Depending an whether or not Venus is favourably aspected, this situation may either make the spouse suffer or make him inflict the same. It may also indicate a rich matrimonial alliance. However due to the infidelity of either one of the partners, there is no harmony, accord or peace.

The planet also endows the native with vigour, morality and bravery, all of which enable him to prosper, provided Mercury is well placed.

In 10° of Taurus, the situation of Mars is wicked since it is the cause for violence, injuries, estrangement and envy.

In 20° of Taurus, the planet brings many emotional problems, resulting in sadness in the home, particularly in the 4th House. In the 3rd or 9th House, it indicates some travel in relation to a love affair and this shall be the product of a reckless act bringing sadness.

Astro Advice

* Donate wheat and *sarson* oil on Tuesday evening 41 minutes before sunset.

Mars in Gemini

When placed in Gemini and favourably aspected by Mercury, Mars is a definite indicator of the native being an interesting conversationalist, agile, intelligent, and able to manage the chart of his life in order to prosper.

This situation, frequently, leads to a tendency to make friends easily. However, the feelings do not run deep. The native is soft hearted. However his generosity is spread out. His warm voice earns him many friends and leads him to prosper as a lawyer, politician or businessman. From the academic perspective this situation is beneficial in the 3rd House, since the native will have the ability to learn a lot. When in the 6th or 12th House, the planet signifies the threat of an injury to a limb of the native.

When in 10° of Gemini, Mars bestows a sensitive, somewhat hot-headed temperament and cardiac problems. In the 8th House, this planet threatens the native with an unexpected demise, particularly through angina pectoris. The native has a tendency to get stressed rather than face actual hurdles and his pessimism shall be towards issues ruled by the House in which Mars is placed.

In 20° of Gemini, the planet endows masculinity and physical strength. If Jupiter is favourably aspected, this situation is beneficial for the House occupied by Gemini.

Astro Advice

• Go for *Tula Daan* of seven grains.

Mars in Cancer

In Cancer, the planet is not very favourably situated. It indicates a native who is a braggart and who lacks the ability to implement his ideas, unless the adverse influence is scattered by favourable aspects from other planets. With such beneficial aspects, the planet endows phases of recklessness rather than actual bravery. The native does not understand danger. There is a great deal of aspiration and ambition and if Jupiter is well placed, it will get quick success and sudden and easy profits.

When in 10° of Cancer, Mars will bring unknown adversaries who shall cause a lot of harm to the native. When Mars is in a square aspect to Saturn, it indicates a severe mishap and signifies fatality if the aspect is in the 8th House with Sun adversely placed.

When in 20° of Cancer, the planet brings bouts of violence that are hard to overwhelm. However the native is honest and to the point. If situated in a House that is not beneficial this can result in severe stomach disorders with vomiting of blood as a result of a stomach wound or ulcer.

Astro Advice

• Donate *gur* every Tuesday at a religious place.

Mars in Leo

This is a beneficial position which allows the native to dominate others and exercise self-control. The analytical skills of the native are of a high order and he also has an intelligence that is energetic and vigorous. It signifies adversaries, who may be strong, and rivals who will try to hurt him but will not manage to do so. In the 8th House, it signifies unexpected demise due to cardiac illness. In the 1st House, it indicates an eye injury in the native's childhood. Mars in this sign bestows generosity and flexibility, however, very little tolerance. The native desires to be listened to at once.

Mars in 10° of Leo makes the native straightforward, so much so that he impulsively tells other people about his plans and schemes. This carelessness and unfocused nature may harm him. He wishes to assist others, however he can also be nosey and interfering.

When in 20° of Leo, the planet brings hard-earned prosperity. There exists the possibility of hurdles and injuries despite which the native shall succeed.

Astro Advice

- Seek the blessings of your parents daily.

Mars in Virgo

In this sign, Mars makes the native highly pessimistic and negative. He is not content with what he has and is extremely critical. He opposes everything and will not have enduring relationships. He will lead a secluded life and marriage shall be bleak and dismal unless Venus is favourably situated in this chart. Unfavourably situated, Mars results in difficulties in realising any goal. The native shall be unlucky in matters of the heart generally due to his own mistakes and he will lead a sad life without any offsprings or loving relationships.

In 10° of Virgo, Mars is highly unfavourable. Nothing goes right with the native unless Jupiter is favourably aspected.

In 20° of Virgo, if Venus is strong, the native shall enter into matrimony and if Mars is situated in an angular House, it will benefit him financially.

Astro Advice

• Fast on full moon days.

Mars in Libra

Mars in Libra endows the native with an immense amount of intellect and energy which will be beneficial for creative endeavours and even if the native is not an artist, he will definitely have aesthetic tastes. This situation endows him with determination in order to overcome hardships and hurdles. Emotionally, the native shall have a good amount of sentimentality which may not always be respected. If the planet is situated in the 7th House and Jupiter is afflicted, separation is certain.

When in 10° of Libra, Mars gives the native an excellent mental faculty and comprehension which will give him the ability to be a good conversationalist. This situation also gives prosperity in a profession wherein the native is his own boss.

When in 20° of Libra, the planet bestows wealth and material riches. In the 5th House, the planet may cause the loss of an offspring, if Saturn is aspected adversely.

Astro Advice

- Donate clothes to Brahmins on your birthday.

Mars in Scorpio

Mars in Scorpio is a sign of many problems and hardships which will be overcome only if Mercury is influential. The native shall be required to be more clever and capable than aggressive. The native however shall be forceful and shrewd. He shall have many adversaries and will have the threat of injuries hanging over his head. In the 6th House, this situation may cause chest ailments if the Moon is afflicted and if Saturn and Venus are in adverse aspect, then tuberculosis.

The planet will benefit business ventures related to poisons or other chemicals.

When in 10° of Scorpio, the planet bestows a lot of vigour and vitality. If the Sun is favourably placed, it will enable the native to live to a ripe old age. In the 10th House, he will pursue many career paths simultaneously.

In 20° of Scorpio, it indicates infidelity and disloyalty unless Venus is favourably placed, or else, an aggressive and regrettable act may take place.

Astro Advice

- Donate eatables to an orphanage.

Mars in Sagittarius

When Mars is situated in Sagittarius, it is a highly beneficial situation since it gives the native kindness, fidelity, benevolence and also the ability to attain a high post by virtue of his own efforts and intellect. In the 6th House, health may be delicate and there may be death before the native reaches 40, unless Jupiter is influential.

In 10° of Sagittarius, the planet makes the native prosper and conquer hardships easily.

In 20° of Sagittarius, profits are earned only if Mercury is favourably positioned since an adverse aspect will result in losses.

Astro Advice

• Avoid drinks on Wednesdays.

Mars in Capricorn

Mars situated in Capricorn signifies a problematic life. Frequent travel and alterations in posts shall mark the native's life who himself will be inconstant and highly capricious. If Saturn is favourably positioned, he shall be pampered by luck and wealth. If Saturn is weak and Capricorn is not situated in a favourable House, Mars in this sign will result in severe leg injuries.

When aspected favourably, the native is understanding. He will have an impressive persona and will mingle with powerful people.

When in 10° of Capricorn the planet makes the native agile, clever and flexible. His personality may not be all that attractive, however his prosperity will remain unaffected as long as Moon and Jupiter are favourably positioned. If the Sun or Moon is feeble and adversely aspected with Mars in the 8th House, it signifies a serious threat to life.

In 20° of Capricorn, the planet signifies frequent travel, particularly if this happens in either the 3rd or 9th House, which are the Houses of travel. This also signifies strength and health. In the 8th House, it indicates a mishap resulting in death at a place away from the native's residence.

Astro Advice

• Get up early in the morning and offer water to the rising sun.

Mars in Aquarius

When Mars is situated in Aquarius, it indicates that the native will be gentle, generous, obstinate and with a tendency towards a fiery temper. When in the 6th House, Mars causes illnesses like asthma, rheumatism and other leg complaints.

When in 10° of Aquarius, there exists the probability of being cheated in issues ruled by the House in which Aquarius is situated.

In 20° of Aquarius, the situation is beneficial for the mind and if Uranus is favourably positioned in the chart, it will enable the native to think of an innovative idea that will help him in getting out of sticky situations.

Astro Advice

• Offer water to Tulsi every morning.

Mars in Pisces

This situation indicates a person who will occupy a medium level position such as a government official, business person, worker. He will enjoy the company of those who are in a better position than him and this will help him in difficult times. He is stable, careful and balanced.

His sense of thrift will ensure that he will have a good income to support himself.

When in 10° of Pisces, the planet endows the native with a lot of energy and a strong, healthy disposition. However, in matters of love and marriage, it indicates cheating and infidelity of the spouse.

In 20° of Pisces, the planet brings progress at a slow but steady pace and the hard work and perseverance of the native shall earn him a secure, stable position, devoid of stress or worry.

Astro Advice

• Donate copper utensils to the poor.

Saturn

Saturn is an arid, infertile and cold planet. Its day domicile is in Aquarius and night is in Capricorn. It is farther from the Earth in Sagittarius and closest in Gemini. It is exiled in Leo and Cancer. It is exalted in 21° of Libra, its fall is in Aries and its joy is in Capricorn.

Saturn's metal is lead and colour is a deep green. Its day is Saturday. It affects the digestive system and the bone structure and endows the native with good height, a pallid skin and brown hair.

Characteristically, it makes the individual cynical, arrogant, calm, hardworking and careful. It also bestows him with a logical, scientific bent of mind. Materially, it tends to affect property issues.

It is referred to as the Great Misfortune and its adverse aspects to the other planets and Houses are very bad when it is negatively placed in the horoscope. However, if its placement is strong, it might result in immense prosperity.

Saturn is responsible for delaying things. It is prudent yet slow and indicates firmness and stability as long as it is beneficially aspected.

Under the effect of Saturn, the subject may have a long life but marked with many severe diseases.

In a layout of cards, it denotes good advice, arrogance, old age and patience.

SATURN IN THE HOUSES

Saturn in the First House

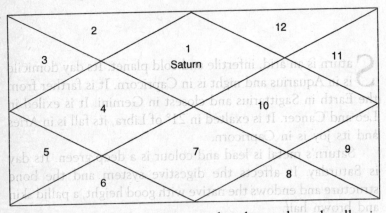

When situated in the 1st House, the planet places hurdles in the path of the native during his youth. It endows him with a self-reliant, profound and solitary mind. It also gives him the desire to study and acquire new knowledge and ideas. It signifies a child who may not be talented but is hardworking and coupled with his self esteem, will make him earn top honours in exams and tests. If the planet is favourably aspected, it will allow the native to reach a high post, though after some hardships.

Astro Advice

- Donate oil and black *til*.

Saturn in the Second House

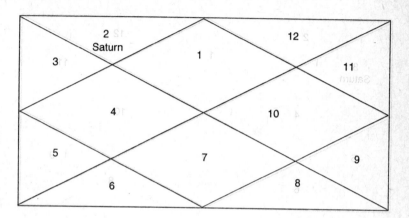

Placed in the 2ⁿᵈ House, Saturn is unfavourable for matters related to money and the personal worth of the native. The native should not indulge in business or trade since he is not suited for it. This situation results in the decline of an individual's status and wealth.

It is clear that the favourable aspects of Venus, Jupiter and the Sun, will remove the negativity. However, prosperity will be achieved only through hard work, thrift and determination.

If favourably aspected by Mercury, it indicates that wealth may be invested securely.

Astro Advice

- Avoid wearing black clothes.

Saturn in the Third House

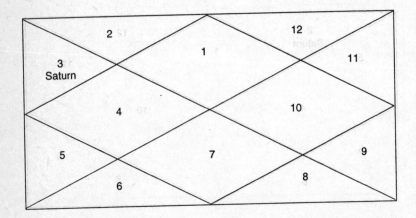

When situated in the 3rd House, the planet causes the delayed development of the native's personality. In childhood, the native is lonely and hesitant. If Saturn is negatively placed and adversely aspected by Mercury, he may acquire wrong habits which may go on to harm his health. If the 6th House is also negatively affected, as an adult, the native will not have a vast social circle. He will remain with family members and some acquaintances. This situation results in arguments and is not good for undertaking journeys. If favourably aspected by Mercury, the native will have a scientific bent of mind.

Astro Advice

- Give full respect to guests and in-laws.

Saturn in the Fourth House

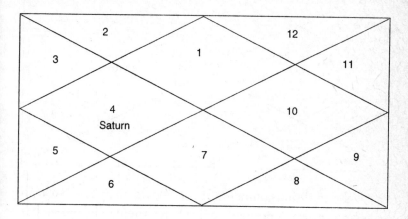

Placed in the nadir of Heavens, the planet when favourably aspected endows the native's family with stability and good heritage. It signifies property and the native will have a considerable legacy. If Saturn is feeble or negatively aspected, all of the above will be reversed and substituted by arguments with one's parents and elders. It will result in a sad marriage and domestic life. The native will lead a lonely life devoid of love and relationships.

Astro Advice

• High class Sapphire of six *rattis* is your lucky stone.

Saturn in the Fifth House

Saturn, when situated in the 5th House of Pleasures is not in its justified position. There is a lack of accord and it will only

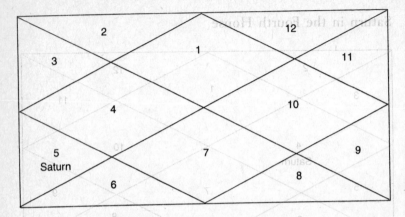

bring about disillusionment. It signifies a marriage with no offspring or else, a premature death for them. The native has an inclination to speculate; however, he is extremely unfortunate. The planet tries its luck, however, is unable to exercise it, particularly, if adversely aspected by Mars. This placement endows the native with strange preferences to earn enjoyment. In a water sign, such as Pisces or Cancer, it makes the native untidy and lazy.

Astro Advice

• Recite the following *mantra* 108 times in the morning at 8.00 a.m.:
  'Aum Shran Shrin Shron Sai Shana Charaye Namah'.

Saturn in the Sixth House

When placed in the purgatory of the Zodiac system, this planet brings about an increase in the problems affecting

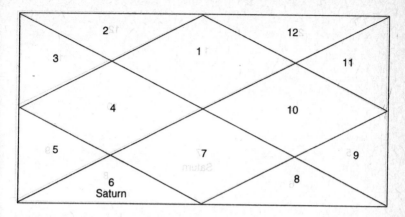

humanity. It brings all sorts of hardships and problems. There is lack of domestic accord; health is endangered and it frequently causes severe illnesses related to tissue.

If Saturn is dignified in the 6th House, it might bestow financial security but an average job. An adverse aspect of Mercury will result in problems with the domestic help or employees while that of the Moon will cause disputes with relatives over a legacy.

Astro Advice

- Prayer to sun, Lord Shiva or Hanuman will bring excellent results.

Saturn in the Seventh House

Saturn in the 7th House results in sadness in matrimony, particularly, in a female horoscope since it refers to a self-centred and envious spouse. It also indicates that the native

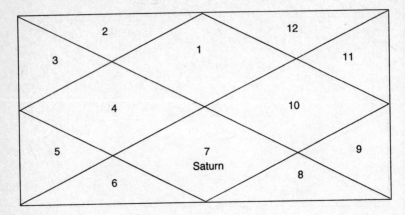

will have a late marriage and that his spouse will either be a widow or older than him.

If the planet is favourably aspected and well dignified, it indicates a happy marriage. However, the native's partner may die an untimely death.

The 7th House affects business alliances and Saturn is not very favourably placed herein. If an alliance does occur, the planet refuses to bow down and the partnership breaks up rapidly, may be through a court case, if adversely aspected by the Sun.

Astro Advice

• Donate black *til*.

Saturn in the Eighth House

Saturn in the 8th House is a favourable position for a long and fruitful life if the Sun is strong in the horoscope. It brings

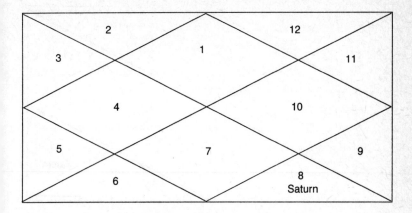

difficulties with regard to legacies after the death of the spouse or one of the parents.

This situation may result in a severe illness and an adverse aspect of Mars may cause the untimely and early demise of the father.

When adversely aspected, it denotes marriage with a poor person or financial difficulties after getting married.

Astro Advice

• Go for *Tula-Daan* of oil or foodgrains.

Saturn in the Ninth House

In this House, the planet makes the native an idealist and a dreamer. However, a favourable aspect may make his thoughts more profound. This is a good situation for one engaged in politics. It endows a dislike for travel and a preference for slow and sedate habits. The native is prudent and depending upon

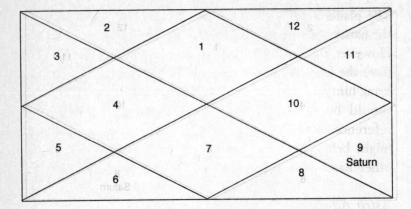

the signs of the 3rd House, he might make an astute lawyer, religious head or academician.

Astro Advice

- To guard against witchcraft you should offer foodgrains, blankets and oil in charity on Saturday evenings.

Saturn in the Tenth House

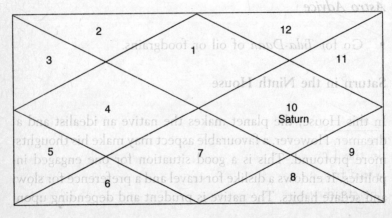

The planet is favourably situated in this House and endows the native with a high character, noble aspirations and success. However, there will be fluctuations in his prosperity. He may have the highest position. However, unforeseen events may bring him down to the bottom. The planet in the 10th House should be examined with great care, particularly with reference to the aspects since it is a crucial situation and might bring about the loss of all that is earned, or on the other hand stabilise the financial status of the native.

Astro Advice

- A ring of eight gems in eight metals will prove beneficial.

Saturn in the Eleventh House

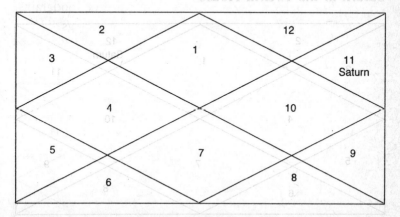

In the 11th House, Saturn does not allow the native to have a vast friend circle. He does not make friends easily. However, the steadiness of his feelings can be depended upon. He may have only a few friends but they will be loyal and hold high posts which will assist the native and he may connect his prosperity with theirs.

This situation does not bless the native with many children. His offsprings will be sensitive, and if they survive they will rise to great heights by virtue of their father's repute and friend circle.

If the planet is negatively aspected it is unfortunate for the offspring and may also result in the native being cheated by a friend in matters related to the aspects of the planet.

Astro Advice

• Immerse 21 black nails in flowing water.

Saturn in the Twelfth House

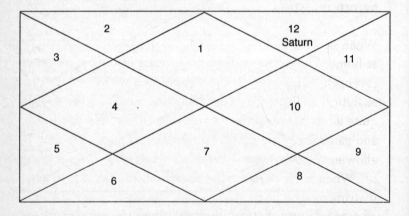

Saturn, when situated in this extremely unlucky House, will have a negative influence. All issues will be affected and harmed by this position. It will result in the downfall of money and status, separation, death, loneliness, mental problems.

If the planet is favourably aspected in the sign which is in the 12th House, nothing bad will take place. Growth may not be significant, yet the native will have a secure and steady life and peace will be there by virtue of his own hard work and carefulness. The last days of his life may be lonely but not unlucky or sad.

Astro Advice

- Recite the following *mantra* 108 times:
  'Aum Pran Prin Pron Sae Shanicharaye Namah.'

SATURN IN THE SIGNS

Saturn in Aries

When situated in Aries, the planet is not favourable for accord at home. The native is stubborn, overtly critical, arrogant and revengeful. However, he is also bestowed with fine logical and analytical abilities. Growth will not be easy, and there will be quite a few hardships in life and an inclination for speculation and gambling. This particular situation is responsible for not allowing the individual to establish his standing at an early age.

When in 10° of Aries, the planet causes a delay in receiving matrimony. It is an indication of disillusionment in love affairs or estrangement, which may not be permanent provided the planet is favourably aspected. If the Sun is positively placed, it bestows prosperity and a high position.

When in 20° of Aries, the planet is extremely unfavourable. It causes numerous problems which the native exaggerates, thereby resulting in great anxiety. This placing is not very good for health, particularly in the 6th and 12th House.

Astro Advice

• Donate blankets to the poor.

Saturn in Taurus

Placed in Taurus, Saturn causes an imbalance of the senses. It indicates a tendency towards bad habits on the part of either the native or his friends, depending upon the Houses that Taurus occupies. Feelings and emotions are ruled more by the mind than the heart. This situation gives the opportunity to prosper through a woman.

The native enjoys being on his own and is wise and thrifty. He shall be able to retain his status by virtue of his own work, if his occupation demands the use of mind power.

Saturn in the 6th or 12th House indicates that the individual may be prone to some infectious illness. In the 8th House, it signifies the father's early demise.

When in 10° of Taurus, the planet causes disease of the senses which may harm the native's health. Also, the native will be envious and not well-balanced, all of which will harm him greatly.

Astro Advice

• Donate black clothes to a sweeper.

Saturn in Gemini

Situated in Gemini, the planet gives the native the mind of an inventor with the ability to be technical, particularly if it is favourably aspected by Mars. This position signifies that other people may be jealous of the native. When in 10° of Gemini, the native has a restless mind. He lacks confidence, optimism and tends to blow everything out of proportion.

When in 20° of Gemini, the native is gentle and patient. He accepts whatever comes his way and is so complacent that he does not act so to achieve fame and fortune.

Astro Advice

• Immerse *Saboot Mah* in flowing water.

Saturn in Cancer

Saturn situated in Cancer is not a favourable position since when this planet is situated in the Moon's domicile, it causes some imbalance or makes the native unsure and unsteady mentally.

When in the 6th House, it causes disorders of the bladder, kidney or stomach and there is a threat from water or liquids.

In this position, the planet is not beneficial for prosperity and hampers the schemes of the native causing drastic changes in his financial state.

When in 10° of Cancer there exists the threat of mishaps while on a journey. If the placing is in the 4th or the 7th House, it signifies disputes with spouse or family member. An adverse aspect of Mars will result in fatal accidents while travelling, particularly if this aspect is in the 8ᵗʰ House.

When in 20° of Cancer, the situation is somewhat favourable yet not very secure. There may be some phases of good fortune because of this decanate's favourable aspects. However, Saturn still has an adverse effect and results in evil deeds related to matters ruled by the House in which the sign is situated.

Astro Advice

• Donate cement to the place of worship.

Saturn in Leo

Not very fortunate for marriage, as this planet causes the separation of the marriage partners and sometimes divorce.

The disposition of the native is alternately too reserved or else too talkative; the mind is quick and intelligent, but not always kind. There may even be a tendency towards spitefulness, especially in a feminine horoscope, and this does not tend to attract sympathy. Nothing succeeds in life, there is continual strife, disappointment and vexation. It is a position which causes its native to be constantly buffeted by fate.

The native loses his happiness, is ever worried, loses his sense of proportion and mental equilibrium and is weak in all respects, having a thin and lean body which is a characteristic of Saturn.

Astro Advice

• Donate black wine.

Saturn in Virgo

There is a suggestion of moral loneliness, and with evil aspects it may lead to suicide. This position is not good for marriage, and in any case the union is childless. There is much intuition, the ideas are lofty, and thoughts of the beyond haunt the native, who is interested in occultism.

Saturn causes physical and moral weakness. The native encounters a destiny against which he can do nothing except wait for better days to come.

The house is also evil for Saturn to occupy. It denies him intelligence and children which one normally gets if this house is favourably occupied or aspected. As intelligence is also denied, he loses discretion, tact and a sense of proportion in his dealings with others. The Saturnine aspect of the house which is the house of his wife's sexual relations may as well lead to his wife having secret sexual relations with some Saturnine person.

Astro Advice

• Donate *sarson* oil.

Saturn in Libra

Saturn gives good mental faculties, and a taste for knowledge. The mind develops, but unfortunately the worldly position does not do likewise, and it remains precarious.

Saturn is very powerful and is not malefic. If the luminaries and the benefic planets are well situated in the horoscope, this position may procure a steady and eminent position in life, but it is nonetheless unfortunate for marriage as there are no children, or else the children are delicate. In any case, there is always some trouble connected with them.

If Saturn is in the house of enemies, the native becomes prominent among philanthropists, illustrious, a king, always conquering groups of his enemies but remaining ever worried.

Astro Advice

• Offer water to the rising sun.

Saturn in Scorpio

Anger and passion are mitigated by the desire to succeed through cunning and ambition so that the beneficial aspects of Mars, among others, will give a daring which may bring success if the luminaries are well situated.

Saturn in Scorpio gives a long life, good health and the possibility of success through the native's skill, tactfulness, industry and intelligence.

Little good can be expected when this occurs in Rahu. There will be many illnesses, which will not be fatal, but which mar the native's life. Saturn brings the risk of close confinement, of dementia. It is a sign of severe illness, or more probably of an accident which may endanger life or cause a wound which will leave painful scars.

If Saturn is in Scorpio, the native is unintelligent, of bad character, of lean and thin body, reserved in speech and ever subordinate. The Saturnine aspect on the ascendant makes the native lean and thin and reticent; he/she does not talk much.

Astro Advice

• Seek the blessings of your parents.

Saturn in Sagittarius

The native always maintains a calm attitude, without unnecessary words or gestures.

There will be many changes of position and of residence, also many illicit unions. Position in general will be established late in life.

Success will be difficult to achieve. The goal aimed at is remote in consequence of the native's own ambition. Good influence will help him to obtain his desires, which are anything but modest. As he is energetic, industrious and persevering, however, as well as honest and kind, there is no reason why he should not succeed.

Sagittarius is again an evil house for Saturn to occupy. From this position he aspects the 10th House (house of profession), the 2nd House of finance and the 5th House (house of intelligence). The 8th House being the house of danger to life, the native obviously suffers in health and remains sickly.

Astro Advice

• Women are advised to take bath in water mixed with honey.

Saturn in Capricorn

The native's integrity will attract many influential friends, who will help him in his undertakings. In this sign, Saturn also denotes the acquisition of house and property.

In the 6th, 8th to 12th Houses, Saturn causes a chequered career, with many ups and down till the end of life.

The exile of Jupiter and of the Moon is necessary in order that something fortunate should occur. Jupiter should be well placed, in which case, with a good aspect of Mercury, success will be notable, although it is also necessary for the Moon to be well placed.

Saturn bestows a long life and if Mars is well situated, the native will be free from illnesses.

Saturn in its own house of Capricorn is the best trinal house where both benefics and malefics offer beneficial results. From this house, Saturn aspects the house of gains and hence the native becomes wealthy, prosperous, kind and sweet-tongued. His wishes are fulfilled. But he is bound to face periodic obstacles in his progress.

Astro Advice

•   Donate gold, emeralds, *ghee*, green clothes and foodgrains for overall prosperity.

Saturn in Aquarius

It is an angular house. Saturn promises a notable rise in life, an exalted position, and a remunerative job around the fortieth year. The native is kind, quiet, reserved, prudent, industrious; his ideas are lofty, he is very magnetic. Being endowed with great power of persuasion he will obtain help and sympathy from everyone. If on the contrary, the day luminary is in good aspect, Saturn will give a long and carefree life. The native is very original, independent, stately and kind. He is noble minded, and his progress will be slow but steady; it will reach its zenith towards the forty-fifth year.

If Saturn is in the royal house with Aquarius, the native becomes a king or a king's adviser, respected, prosperous, performing good deeds of a loving nature and ever happy.

Astro Advice

• Donate black clothes.

Saturn in Pisces

This position is far from fortunate. Saturn in Pisces gives a great tendency towards melancholy and morbidity. The temper is changeable and thoughts of suicide may haunt the native. Disappointments are connected with affection and with children.

When marriage takes place there is not much security, as one of the partners can deceive the other.

The benefic nature of Saturn endows the native with a handsome appearance, lean body, sweet tongue, kind heartedness and patience. The native suffers because of generosity.

Astro Advice

• Donate *Saboot Mah* at place of worship.

Rahu

Rahu is a shadowy and supernatural planet. It is similar to Saturn, Mars and sometimes Jupiter. Deep blue in colour, Aquarius is its abode, Leo its exile, Scorpio its exaltation and Taurus is its fall. Cold and barren in nature, it influences the mind, the nervous system and the brain, corresponding to its placement in the horoscope, house and sign of the native, it causes uncommon and abnormal events. Under its influence the native acts like a maniac, a psychic or an executrix radiating electro-magnetic waves. Its deep repercussions on human life as a whole can be unexpectedly disastrous and catastrophic. The planet overall is a symbol of selfishness, troubles and plays a very decisive part in the native's life in accordance with its placement in house, sign and aspects.

RAHU IN THE HOUSES

Rahu in the First House

Rahu in the 1ˢᵗ House of the native gives him a place of distinction, a known man whether good or bad. The native has

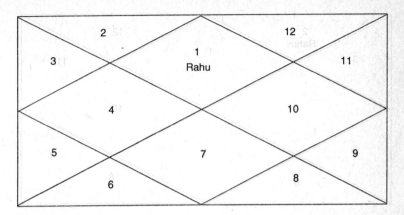

convictions of his own. He is original and peculiar, stubborn and self-willed in mind, unwilling to submit to reason or control. It might shock people around but unmindful of their reaction, the native achieves a notable position in a profession though after great struggle. Generally marked by intense desire for advancement for name, fame, wealth and power, the native is a master as he would always strive, never satisfied with himself. Under malefic influence, he revolts against the established norms. His thoughts are chaotic and action is full of hatred and spirit of revenge. Rahu shapes the native into a self-centred and egoistic being.

Astro Advice

• Do not keep broken utensils at home.

Rahu in the Second House

Rahu in the 2nd House is not good for business affairs as it is not flexible enough to enable the native to bend to the caprice

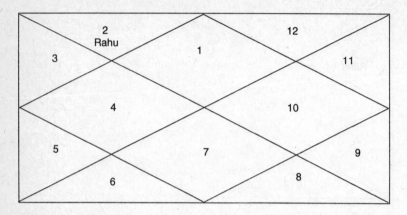

of a customer. It brings sudden alterations, great losses and unexpected gains.

If Rahu is in the 2nd House the person ceases to perform religious and other good deeds, suffers troubles and difficulties due to his own action and becomes happy after earning money in a foreign place.

Astro Advice

• Give food to animals.

Rahu in the Third House

This position is auspicious for the native's mentality and will help him in his profession as it enables him to draw the attention of his associates to himself. This position is also an indication of travelling, as the native cannot remain for long in the same place. The native leads a pure life armed with a king's authority. He is illustrious, influential, happy, wealthy

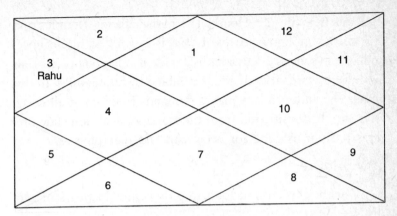

and charitably disposed. In this position the native becomes religious minded, leading a happy life, in contradistinction to the unhappy one by its position in the 2nd House.

Astro Advice

• Pray to your deity every morning.

Rahu in the Fourth House

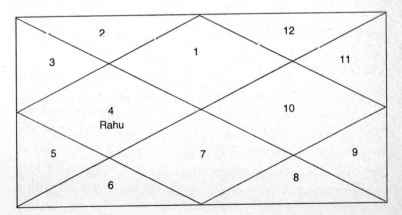

If Rahu is in the 4th House, the native, facing troubles and difficulties at home leaves it. He is devoid of intelligence, indulges in useless discussions, is deprived of happiness, remains inimical towards friends and is troubled by his enemies. In this house this independent planet demands freedom at all costs. It is very badly situated from the standpoint of domestic life. This position is good for occultism and metaphysics.

Astro Advice

• Donate clothes and food to girls below 11 years of age.

Rahu in the Fifth House

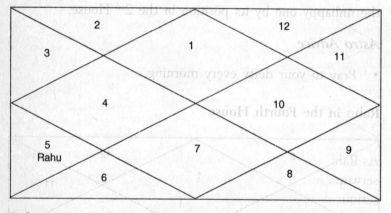

Rahu is not well placed in this house, in which it upsets material welfare. If this planet is in a fruitful sign, it is an indication of trouble connected with childbirth. The children may die young, and death may often be due to meningitis. In the affliction of this house, the native not only loses the capacity to earn but could also be faced with a flirtatious wife and in the absence of his own ability to produce children, he has to tolerate his wife's conduct and this may force him to be indifferent towards the family.

Astro Advice

• Avoid taking bribes.

Rahu in the Sixth House

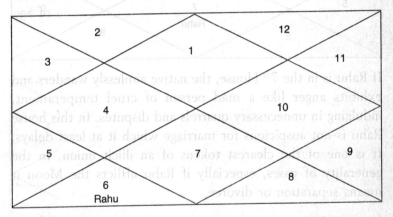

As Rahu always makes a leader, this position in the house of servants and employees is not favourable, causing, as it does, serious disputes with subordinates. The native becomes very rich through such a source, acquires political/judicial power from such a government and subdues his enemies. The last is the normal trait of any malefic in the 6th House.

Astro Advice

• **Always speak the truth.**

Rahu in the Seventh House

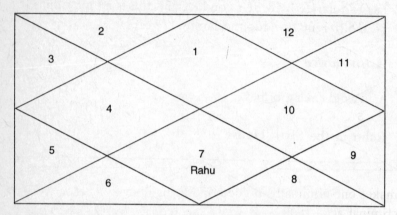

If Rahu is in the 7th House, the native aimlessly wanders and exhibits anger like a mad person of cruel temperament, indulging in unnecessary quarrels and disputes. In this house Rahu is not auspicious for marriage which it at least delays. It is one of the clearest tokens of an illicit union. In the generality of cases, especially if Rahu afflicts the Moon it means separation or divorce.

Astro Advice

• Offer milk to moneyplant at home.

Rahu in the Eighth House

If Rahu is in the 8th House, the native becomes stout in body, wanders in foreign places, is short-tempered, poor and does evil acts. Rahu's aspect in the 2nd House deprives the native of wealth and makes him poor. Mars in combination with Rahu

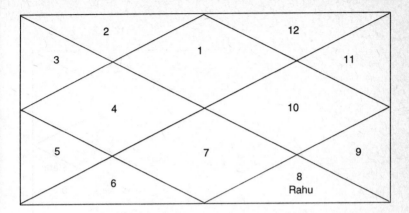

makes one criminally minded, indulging in evil or unsociable, criminal acts. If Rahu is well aspected, it gives a possibility of gain from matters connected with funerals or a pronounced taste for things connected with death. As with Rahu in the 1st House, this position in the 8th House gives a desire for solitude.

Astro Advice

• See your palm daily in the morning.

Rahu in the Ninth House

If Rahu is in the house of fate, the native is blessed with jewels of various kinds, brocaded dresses, a large number of servants and is generally happy. It makes the native the leader of a school of thought, a man who expects others to adopt his own ideas, also a man who creates new methods, whether scientific or philosophical.

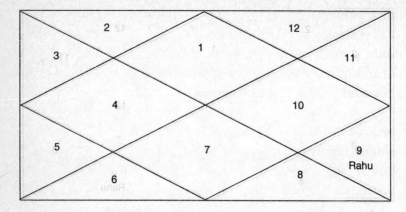

In this house of long journeys, Rahu is favourable for travelling but this will not occur without trouble, as such journeys will always be adventurous and undertaken without due preparation.

Astro Advice

- Prayer to the sun and Vishnu is beneficial. It is good for life and prosperity.

Rahu in the Tenth House

This is one of the best positions for Rahu to occupy. Hence he confers on the native health, wealth, affluence, prosperity, benevolence and freedom from enemies and worries or, in other words, full enjoyment of the pleasures of the world as any popular king would wish to. This position is very favourable for those who wish to take up occultism. With bad aspect, it is most unfavourable, causing constant changes and alterations

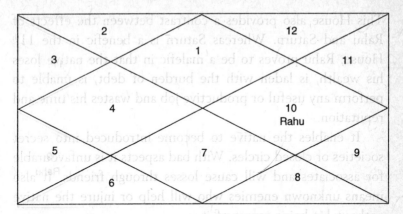

in life. It is often a sign of inability to succeed in worldly matters.

Astro Advice

- Prayer to Ganesha will give you strong intuitive power and peace of mind.

Rahu in the Eleventh House

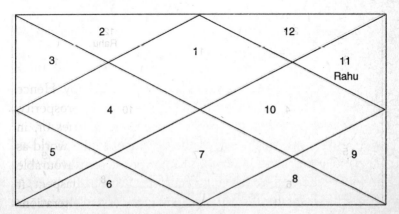

This House also provides a contrast between the effects of Rahu and Saturn. Whereas Saturn is a benefic in the 11th House, Rahu proves to be a malefic in that the native loses his wealth, is laden with the burden of debt, is unable to perform any useful or productive job and wastes his time and reputation.

It enables the native to become introduced into secret societies or closed circles. With bad aspects it is unfavourable for associates and will cause losses through friends. It also means unknown enemies who will help or injure the native without his being aware of it.

Astro Advice

- For better results recite the following *mantra*:
  'Aum Bhran Bhrin Bhron Sae Rahve Namah.'

Rahu in the Twelfth House

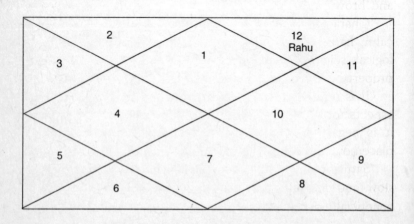

This is a natural malefic house and the person loses his wealth, loves quarrels and disputes, is burdened with debt and is an aimless wanderer.

In this position, if well aspected with the luminaries, there is a likelihood of gain in secret occupations, money being acquired without trouble and with little exertion. This planet in the 12th House is not good for a public occupation, even if it is dignified.

A bad aspect of Mercury with Rahu means theft or unpaid debts, serious pecuniary troubles which may cause loss of position.

Astro Advice

• Your favourable direction is west.

RAHU IN THE SIGNS

Rahu in Aries

Arians tend to become independent, self-witted, courageous and of firm convictions. The native craves for change, for continuous attainments in life to acquire name and fame. If Rahu is favourably aspected till 10° of Aries, he attains the desires of his heart and turns fortune favourably making him a distinguished person. Rahu in 20° of Aries is very harmful and destructive. In this position the fallout of the planet depends upon the house occupied by the sign i.e. loss of position in the 10th House, separation in marriage in the 7th House etc., and illness or sudden fit of anger and subsequent skirmish in the 6th House.

Astro Advice

- You are advised to avoid black colour.

Rahu in Taurus

Taurus sign when occupied by Rahu tends to make the native intuitive, extremely affectionate, obstinate, having faith in goodness of things. The native is sensitive and prone to strange notions about love. Rahu if good in this sign cultivates agricultural interests in the native and gives him success in obtaining produce from land. Rahu in 10° of Taurus is bad for family life as there will be no harmony between the couple and separation will occur if Moon and Venus are not favourably placed.

Rahu in its fall can effect instability (if in 20° of Taurus) depending upon the house it occupies. In this position it denotes mental imbalance or can cause accidents in journeys in the 3rd and 9th House.

Astro Advice

- Avoid fish and alcohol; have a simple diet.

Rahu in Gemini

Geminians draw benefits from Rahu concerning intellectual pursuits when Mercury, Sun and Moon are also well placed. It gives innovative ideas to scientists and engineers. Rahu in Gemini makes scientists go ahead of their times in positive creativity and the native gets monetary benefits too. Rahu gives them inner intellectual abilities. A weak placement of the planet gives poor results making the native imbalanced in his views and thoughts, having unsteady moods and behaviour pattern. A weak Rahu placed in the 6th House can cause psychic disorders especially if malefic Moon aspects the house.

Astro Advice

• Keep a Rahu *Yantra* in your possession.

Rahu in Cancer

Rahu in Cancer is not much desired as it is not helpful especially in the beginning of life. It keeps the native unsettled in his middle age causing frustration, bitterness and depression. This placement of Rahu is bad for marital relations too. It delays marriage and eludes harmony in marriage. In 10° of Cancer, Rahu causes ill-health, stomach disorders, and the danger of accidents is there too, particularly if it is placed in the 6th House.

Astro Advice

• Prayers to Shri Ganpathy or Lord Shiva are helpful.

Rahu in Leo

Rahu is considered good and beneficial in Leo if well aspected. Rahu in the ascendant gives the native a place of pride, a winning look, a liberal heart making the native an undisputed leader, feared, and respected. Rahu in 20° of Leo makes the native successful in establishing his supremacy over his friends and foes alike, but he might not be liked by the members of his family, particularly in the beginning of his life. The native does not get desired harmony from his marriage too, if Rahu is in 10° of Leo. Malefic Sun or Mars in the 7th House along with Rahu may cause separation or divorce.

Astro Advice

- Must wake up before sunrise and offer water/wine to the rising sun.

Rahu in Virgo

Rahu in Virgo renders the native less practical and pragmatic even if the loved sign Virgo is well placed and well aspected. Rahu makes his success in business doubtful, particularly if Rahu is in 10° of Virgo. On the contrary he might succeed in the pursuit of medicine or literary activities resulting in original and creative work. Material gains are delayed. Rahu bestows upon the native a handsome and admirable personality. Rahu in 20° of Virgo in a female native gives her a marital status higher than her standing in life with a comparatively older man. Benefic Moon and Venus with Rahu gives her a happy married life.

Astro Advice

- Chant the following *mantra* 108 times in the morning: 'Aum Hran Hrin Hron Sae Suryaye Namah.'

Rahu in Libra

It is a friendly sign of Rahu hence it endows artistic tastes in the native. The native easily excels in pursuits of art, literature, music, dancing, painting and other fine arts. He wins attainments for his artistic pursuits from the public and attains material comforts too. The originality of his ideas gives him success in whatsoever career and profession he decides to pursue. The native will not be successful in partnerships or joint ventures and malefic influence of Mars may create legal complications and troubles. On the whole, the native rises above his standing and is considered quite successful and intelligent. The evil influence of Mars or Saturn in the 5th House can be unfortunate for the children.

Astro Advice

• Donate black *til*.

Rahu in Scorpio

Rahu in this sign is quite auspicious especially for intellectual pursuits concerning occult sciences. In the 3rd and 9th House it is very favourable and makes the native studious, reserved and self centred. The native tends to adopt immoral means to achieve his ends if Rahu is evil aspected. Rahu in the sign if placed in the 8th House foretells a violent end. In 10° of this sign, benefic Rahu well aspected by Sun and Moon gives good health and a long life. The native may change his profession occasionally. In 20° of Scorpio, Rahu brings troubles especially in the 2nd, 5th or 12th House.

Astro Advice

- Donate rice to brahmin women.

Rahu in Sagittarius

It gives muscular strength and dexterity in sports and different games in case Mars is also beneficent in the horoscope. It gives wisdom, determination, balance, good behaviour, embellished qualities and makes the native successful in his efforts through hurdles and difficulties. It makes the native philosophic and interested in mysticism if in 20° of Sagittarius. The native might emerge as a creator of a new philosophic school.

Astro Advice

- Donate wine.

Rahu in Capricorn

It is not confined to marriage partnerships or joint ventures. The native likes loneliness, indulges in a study of philosophic thoughts or books and loves occult knowledge. He is endowed with leadership qualities if aspected well and can succeed in industry through his persevering and subtle intellect and achieve his aims and objectives. Rahu in 20° of Capricorn may cause serious threats in matters governed by the house it is placed in. Still it favours a long and healthy life.

Astro Advice

• Donate blankets to poor women.

Rahu in Aquarius

Rahu in Aquarius turns the native deeply intellectual, philosophical, a lover of solitude and is good to others only if it is well aspected and well placed. The native attains a high position in life particularly relating to professional dealings with metals or travels. Aquarius in this sign of Saturn is related to metals or travels and Rahu and Saturn are friends. Rahu in Aquarius gives a good harmonious married life. Rahu in 10° of Aquarius may cause some emotional tension but a strong Rahu is favourably disposed to give the native happiness, wealth, prosperity and success depending upon the good position of Venus and Moon.

Astro Advice

• Donate five kinds of grain to a temple.

Rahu in Pisces

It makes a person honest and a frank lover of tours and travels. He is not endowed with much will power and courage but is lucky and fortunate. He belives in the emotion of soul and other philosophical ideas but with Saturn in Pisces he becomes depressed, pessimistic and melancholic . In 10° of Pisces, the native may be immoral and his marriage may break without solid reason. In 20° of Pisces, Rahu ushers fortune and good luck through lotteries and speculations, depending upon the house it occupies.

Astro Advice

- Immerse copper coins in flowing water.

Ketu

Ketu is closely associated with Venus, Moon and the sign
Pisces. Ketu's exile seems to be in Virgo, exaltation in
Cancer and joy in Capricorn. It influences society collectively
rather than individually. So, a horoscope has to be observed
by the influence of other planets vis-a vis their placement in
houses and Ketu may influence the events. It helps touring
and travelling and creates interest in the study of mysticism
and occultism. Under its influence the native tends to become
emotional or of a wavering mind, lazy, vague and indecisive.
If well aspected it brings wealth, good inheritance. However
in matrimonial matters, disharmony and disputes occur under
its influence. The native is often sluggish and suffers from
physical weakness corresponding to the sign it occupies. In
Capricorn, it causes weakness and in Pisces pain in the feet
or lower parts of the body. The emotional pattern of the native
is shaped by Ketu.

KETU IN THE HOUSES

Ketu in the First House

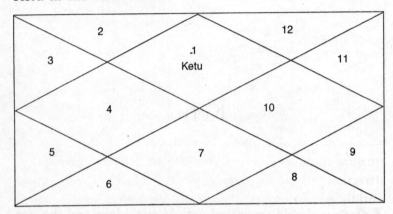

From the health standpoint, the placement of Ketu in the 1st House is inauspicious. The native is left weak, unmanly, lacking vigour and will power. A chronic disease may be caused in that part of the body occupied by this planet. His thought pattern is not based on ground realities rendering him incapable to react against happenings in life. He lacks vigour for physical work.

Astro Advice

- Those suffering from high blood pressure should wear *Rudraksh*.

Ketu in the Second House

If well aspectecd, Ketu is auspicious in this house. The native attains money and success without hardship. His business venture in liquids like milk, juices, etc,. or dealing with eatables

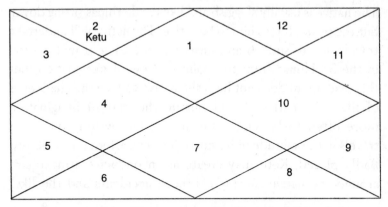

are quite rewarding. He enters wedlock on the basis of physical attraction and the marriage is successful and rewarding from worldly point of view. If malefic, Ketu gives contradictory results i.e. loss of position, status etc.

Astro Advice

• Offer milk, *ghee* to any goddess.

Ketu in the Third House

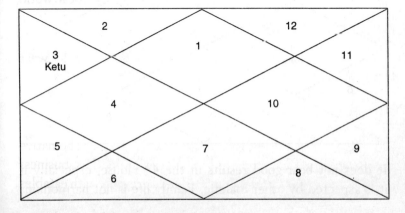

The native is usually sluggish and likes to do things sitting down, but the planet forces him to be active. The native will undertake travels due to sudden and unseen events. The planet is good in the 3rd House from the point of view of imagination, but this placement does not help the native to face the challenges of life. The native should pursue the play of imagination more often to be successful in life, like writing books on travels in the solitude of his home if he can afford it monetarily. Badly placed, Ketu may create an inconducive atmosphere around the native causing conflicts, accidents and the like.

Astro Advice

• Donate sweets to an orphanage.

Ketu in the Fourth House

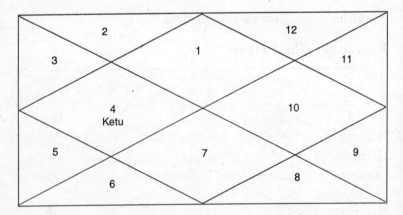

It does not bear good results in the 4th House, especially if it is aspected by other malefic. Family life is not harmonious and children born of such a marriage under the influence of Ketu are unlucky. The native too may not remain in the land of his birth and may die away from it. Well aspected Ketu helps the native favourably in gaining wealth and landed property, a house located near a channel, river or sea.

Astro Advice

• Donate copper utensils to poor men.

Ketu in the Fifth House

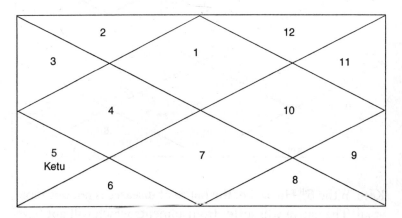

Ketu in the 5th House is beneficial for the birth of children. It tends to make the native emotionally charged which if neglected can damage the native's health. It leads to unwanted, extravagance due to ill organised money matters. Normally the native has friends not in tune with his accomplishments and upbringing, who do not fit into his life and are not conducive for his growth. Afflicted or malefic Ketu tends to make the life partner untrue or insecure and that might damage the reputation of the native, affecting his life and mind.

Astro Advice

- Donate oil, *ghee* or black cloth to a beggar.

Ketu in the Sixth House

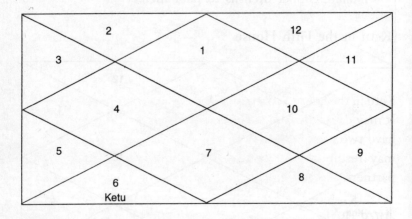

Ketu in the 6th House i.e. the house of diseases is not desirable at all. The native will suffer from ailments which will not have medical solutions. It may cause diseases in the abdomen and concerning growth.

Astro Advice

- Avoid drinks and non-vegetarian food.

Ketu in the Seventh House

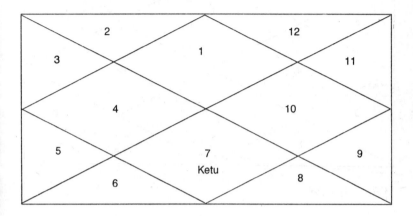

Ketu in the house of partnership and marriage is not auspicious. It may cause divorce and a second marriage or the native may have two living wives. If malefic planets aspect this house, it may result in a loss of wealth, disharmony, disputes with partners and subsequent loss of position.

Astro Advice

• Donate two silver bangles to a brahmin.

Ketu in the Eighth House

Ketu may cause sudden death. The native may acquire good ancestral wealth and property and get married into a wealthy family but may not live long to enjoy his position and inheritance. He may lose his wife too in a short time.

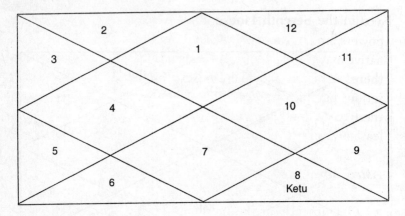

Astro Advice

- Donate curd, camphor in a temple.

Ketu in the Ninth House

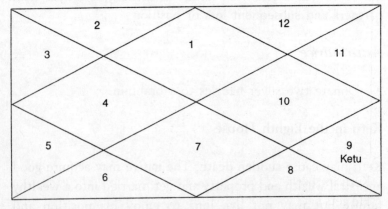

The 9th House when occupied by Ketu, causes deep mental, intellectual pursuits related to philosophies, religious studies or the occult field. The subconscious mind is activated, intuitive powers are increased and visions and dreams come true. The native may travel extensively in alien lands and raise his destiny there. Afflicted and malefic Ketu in this house may cause serious psychic disorders, depressions of the serious type and the like. Malefic Mars can cause death in an alien land or at least away from home.

Astro Advice

- Get up early in the morning.
- Offer water to the rising sun.

Ketu in the Tenth House

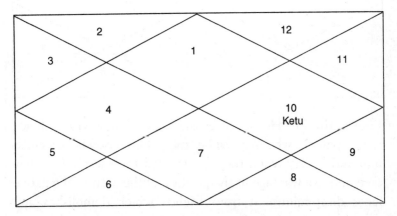

Ketu in the 10th House gives a rewarding place to the native. He gets paid without doing any work suitable to his lazy nature for quite a high office. He may be a manager of some trading association not demanding much labour or head of a shipping concern where he is required to work in a relaxed manner. With malefic Ketu, a reverse position is created concerning his fortunes and family life

Astro Advice

- Immerse empty vessel in flowing water on Sunday after Surya *Puja*.

Ketu in the Eleventh House

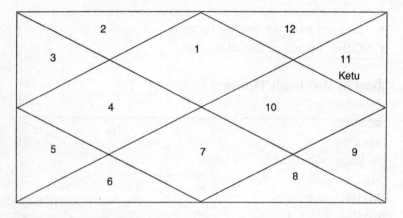

Ketu in the 11th House leaves the native with a wrong choice of companions who may not be true to him. Friends may cheat him and betray when they are needed the most. They may take undue advantage of the position of the native. The native faces disappointment from friends which demolishes and depresses his sensitive nature.

Astro Advice

- Wear Ruby of six *ratti* on ring finger on Sunday morning.

Ketu in the Twelfth House

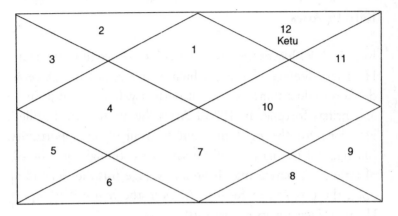

Benefic Ketu in this house brings fortune for the native. Financially the native is in a good position. The native may be successful in the capacity of a religious leader, or a secret agent, or a detective. The native may have interests in knowing about other places, their currency and stamps etc., and have a side business besides his main profession. Malefic and badly aspected Ketu will create enemies, legal battles, frustrations, loss of reputation and a lonely and miserable life.

Astro Advice

- Avoid non-vegetarian food.
- Offer water to the rising sun daily.

KETU IN THE SIGNS

Ketu in Aries

Ketu in Aries leaves the native lethargic, incorrigibly obstinate. He has a feeling of pride which is not apparent. Once he decides to do a thing, he does it perfectly. It is a good position and brings fortune. In 10° of Aries, his wishes are fulfilled. He waits for the right moment to avail of an opportunity. Marriage of the native will be satisfying, though late. In 20° of Aries, the native may have an average fortune depending upon the position of Ketu in Aries in the house it occupies. He may face reverses and misfortunes.

Astro Advice

• Worship womanhood or any goddess.

Ketu in Taurus

The native is helpful, kind and cooperative towards others if it does not cost him much trouble. He has an interest in antique objects. He marries a woman older in age and suffering from some infirmity, sometimes a serious disease of lungs, etc.

In 10° of Taurus, the native has independent ideas but at the same time he is jealous of others, which results in family fights and deadlock.

In 20° of Taurus, it brings pessimism and frustration, travels concerning death of a premature child.

Astro Advice

- Donate seven kinds of grains to a temple according to your weight on your birthday.

Ketu in Gemini

Ketu in Gemini is good from all angles. He will have cooperative friends and he too will be supportive and considerate to the difficulties of his friends and people around.

He is fortunate in acquiring his status in life as well as family affairs, as he is very careful to carry out his duties correctly, very attentive to the minutest details.

Astro Advice

- Give full respect to your elders.
- Touch the feet of your mother daily.

Ketu in Cancer

It is a favourable placement as it tends to give lots of strength and politeness to the native. He surrenders before destiny but is optimistic that a favourable opportunity will come out of the circumstances that have kept him chained. He likes to be rid of difficult situations. He takes an interest in mysticism and hides his real mind from being exposed to others. He will have a happy life only if the planet is well aspected. The house occupied by Ketu in Cancer will bring bad results. Ketu in 10° of Cancer can cause accidents, stomach ailments or diseases in the parts of body ruled by the house. Ketu in 20° of Cancer is exalted but it has to be free from the malefic effect of Mars to give the benefit of the house occupied by the planet.

Astro Advice

- Give *Moong dal* to birds.
- Avoid bad company.

Ketu in Leo

In Leo it is very auspicious from a material outlook. The native will be awarded an administrative position, a distinguished place. He may not lead a group or association but will enjoy the power of the head whose trusted the native can become.

Ketu in 10° of Leo makes the native gregarious, friendly, open-hearted. He may not keep his personal matters to himself and that of others. He is a faithful friend and a life partner.

Neptune in 20° of Leo makes the native quite fortunate, luck always favouring him at the right time. The native may suffer from some health hazards, blood circulation problems, bronchial trouble or some lung problems.

Astro Advice

- Donate silver, milk, rice in a temple.

Ketu in Virgo

In Virgo it tends to make the native revengeful, unforgiving, selfish, greedy and fastidious and not at all kind, friendly or charitable and generous. It may lead to marriage in a wealthy family but with an older women, or it could be a late marriage. If Venus is well placed, the marriage will be happy and lucky.

Astro Advice

• Donate fruits to the blind.

Ketu in Libra

In Libra it renders a carping tongue, strange ideas, mutual disorders marked by extreme excitement, abnormal enthusiasm. Marriage occurs quite late in life, turns unhappy as the couple do not adjust with each other. Neptune in 10° of Libra is good for education especially a technical education like marine engineering, etc. Good placement of Ketu will help the native to discover new things relating to his education. Ketu showers good luck, wealth and material gains in 20° of Libra, provided Mars is benefic. If Mars is afflicted it can damage the house occupied by Ketu.

Astro Advice

• To overcome unexpected loss of money or accident you must weigh yourself for food-grains, black wine, copper-coin and immerse them in flowing water at mid-day.

Ketu in Scorpio

In Scorpio it is liable to make the native artistic, mentally sharp, cunning and skilled, who can improvise crafts according to his designs. Ketu in 10° of Scorpio makes the native interested in medicines and physical disorders concerning females. It can cause health problems or that of the family according to the work occupied by Ketu. Anxiety and mental stress are the other influences caused by Ketu. Evil effects of Rahu may aggravate the influence of Ketu. Weak Venus too adds to anxieties and emotional stress related to women.

Astro Advice

• Donate blankets, oil and blue clothes to the poor.

Ketu in Sagittarius

It is a good position on the whole, as it keeps the native cheerful, kind, generous, benevolent and fond of travel. It makes the native very imaginative, creative, an artist or a writer. In 10° of Sagittarius, the native accomplishes many things through his imagination than in actuality. Good Mars will help him in being successful in life. In 20° of Sagittarius, he is endowed with supernatural powers or witchcraft and the native enjoys interest in magical subjects or other worldly matters. He loves solitude and leads a very frugal life.

Astro Advice

• Give sweet *chapatis* to black dogs for 40 days.

Ketu in Capricorn

The native comes under the influence of others. He is gullible and that will make him miserable sometimes and he may suffer silently. He is not lucky from the worldly point of view, especially in love affairs. Only a good placement of Venus and Moon can save his position. Ketu in 10° of Capricorn is worse depending upon the house it occupies. It damages that aspect of the native governed by the house ruled by it.

Ketu in 20° of Capricorn leaves the native in a little better position concerning fate, activities and physical energy. A good position of Mars in the native's horoscope saves him from physical injuries especially of knees and legs.

Astro Advice

- Tendency to change prayers and worship must be curbed.

Ketu in Aquarius

It makes the native live a peaceful, contented and relaxed life especially from the point of view of family and children. In 10° of Aquarius, it creates troubles for the native though he longs for peace and happiness. These are disturbed rudely, but the stars are kind to him. He finds himself in a comfortable position protected by supernatural powers. If Rahu afflicts Ketu, a sudden misfortune may occur disturbing peace and harmony.

Astro Advice

- Ring of five metals like gold, silver, copper, *kansa* and iron will increase your personal magnetism.

Ketu in Pisces

It is his own abode that gives abundant material resources, a definite income and an easy life. In 10° of Pisces, the native indulges in extra-marital affairs under its influence. He may indulge as he soon gets tired of one and may cause suffering to others, but he himself will not suffer. In 20° of Pisces, he leads a comfortable, peaceful, contented and relaxed life feeling secure about his future.

Astro Advice

• Recite the following *mantra* 108 times in the evening: *'Aum Stran Strin Stron Sae Ketve Namah.'*

The Sun

The following signs for the Sun are: Aries, Cancer, Leo, Scorpio, Sagittarius and Pisces.

Zodiac Sign: Influence of the Sun

Aries: Strong and well-built, aggressive, popular, ambitious, courageous, intelligent.

Taurus: Prominent nose, intelligent, tactful, sociable.

Gemini: Well-proportioned body, learned, wealthy, polite, intelligent, interest in science/ mathematics.

Cancer: Lustful, poor, drunkard, fickle.

Leo: Physically strong, traveller, poor, obstinate, happy-go-lucky.

Virgo: Effeminate, soft-spoken, interest in intellectual pursuits.

Libra: Well-built body, fickle, mean, obstinate, prone to committing bad deeds.

Scorpio: Strong body, bold, cruel, unprincipled, possessing surgical skills.

Sagittarius: Tall, well-proportioned body, wealthy, happy, intelligent, religious, short-tempered.

Capricorn: Thin, small body, stupid, poor, timid, mean, unhappy.

Aquarius: Medium height, poor, base, unfortunate, lustful.

Pisces: Short-statured, rich, religious, learned, loved by the opposite sex.

The Moon

Favourable signs for the Moon are: Taurus, Gemini, Cancer, Leo and Virgo.

Zodiac Sign: Influence of the Moon

Aries: Round eye, sparse hair, bruises on the head, ambitious, lustful, irritable, fickle-minded.

Taurus: Broad chest, curly hair, handsome, popular, respectable, generous, successful, romantic, happy in middle and old age.

Gemini: Projecting nose, black eyes, curly hair, tall, passionate, intelligent, learned, sweet-spoken.

Cancer: Short-statured, charming, wealthy, emotional, happy, intelligent.

Leo: Broad face, reddish eyes, strong body, bold, proud, charitable, unhappy.

Virgo: Attractive modes, reserved, honest, long-armed, drooping shoulders, sweet speech, intelligent, fond of pleasure and the opposite sex.

Libra: Tall, lean, deformed limbs, intelligent, learned, religious, amicable, lover of pleasure and the opposite sex.

Scorpio: Broad eyes, wide chest, well-formed body, mischievous, undependable, straightforward, greedy, wealthy.

Sagittarius: Oval face, long neck, happy, liberal, influential, popular, soft-spoken.

Capricorn:	Thin body and face, clever, crafty, low morals.
Aquarius:	Tall, well formed body, sensual, diplomatic, courteous.
Pisces:	Projecting nose, symmetrical body, soft-spoken, religious, charitable, learned, fond of the opposite sex.

Mercury

The favourable signs for Mercury are: Taurus, Gemini, Leo, Virgo and Libra

Zodiac Sign: Influence of Mercury

Aries:	Lean built, wicked, unscrupulous, deceitful.
Taurus:	Well-built, high position, respectable, moneyed, sensual.
Gemini:	Sweet-spoken, studious, rich, tactful.
Cancer:	Rich, lover of music, sensual, hostile to close relatives.
Leo:	Poor, boastful, unhappy, a wanderer.
Virgo:	Learned, respectable, religious, potential to be an author, generous.
Libra:	Courteous, sociable, philosophical, materialistic, a spendthrift.
Scorpio:	Stupid, miserly, selfish, reckless.
Sagittarius:	Well-built, virtuous, learned, generous, intelligent.
Capricorn:	Miserable, liar, fickle, wicked.
Aquarius:	Poor, quarrelsome, unlucky, unhappy, scholarly.
Pisces:	Devoid of learning, wealth and sons, lover of the opposite sex.

Mars

The favourable signs for Mars are: Aries, Cancer, Leo, Scorpio, Sagittarius and Capricorn.

Zodiac Sign: Influence of Mars

Aries:	Prominent position in military, police or business, rich, happy, sensual, generous.
Taurus:	Immoral, timid, harsh-tongued, unhappy.
Gemini:	Witty, flirtatious, unreliable, sharp-tongued.
Cancer:	Wealthy, intelligent, destined to travel abroad, wicked, possessing weak eyesight.
Leo:	Poor, unsuccessful, unhappy domestic circumstances, interested in astrology, mathematics.
Virgo:	Respectable, affluent, sensuous, extravagant, charming, revengeful.
Libra:	Materialistic, immoral, boastful, deformities in body, quarrelsome.
Scorpio:	Clever, proud, materialistic, diplomatic, passionate.
Sagittarius:	Famous, holding good position, possessing many enemies.
Capricorn:	Wealthy, very good status, generous, influential.
Aquarius:	Poor, untruthful, unlucky, unhappy.
Pisces:	Restless, possessing many enemies, passionate, unprincipled.

Jupiter

The favourable signs for Jupiter are Aries, Cancer, Leo, Scorpio, Sagittarius and Pisces.

Zodiac Sign: Influence of Jupiter

Aries: Wealthy, liberal, bold, intelligent, famous, good status, happy.

Taurus: Wealthy, liberal, popular, polite, happy.

Gemini: Happy, religious, oratorial skills, learned, creative ability.

Cancer: Wealthy, influential, intelligent, famous, respectable, learned, happy.

Leo: Active, brave, ambitious, happy, intelligent.

Virgo: Intelligent, ambitious, affluent, learned, selfish.

Libra: Intelligent, religious, attractive, pleasant.

Scorpio: Proud, zealous, sick, selfish, unhappy.

Sagittarius: Rich, generous, intelligent, influential.

Capricorn: Base, poor, unhappy, tactless, generous.

Aquarius: Greedy, sick, popular, sympathetic, learned, lacking in wealth.

Pisces: Respectable, bold, wealthy, good position.

Venus

The favourable signs for Venus are: Taurus, Gemini, Virgo, Libra, Capricorn, Aquarius and Pisces.

Zodiac Sign: Influence of Venus

Aries:	Immoral, easygoing, extravagant, unhappy.
Taurus:	Popular, rich, handsome, sensuous.
Gemini:	Wealthy, intelligent, sensuous, skilled in arts.
Cancer:	Arrogant, intelligent, unhappy, sensuous.
Leo:	Licentious, procuring money through women, miserable due to his own acts.
Virgo:	Rich, clever, unhappy, lustful.
Libra:	Intelligent, generous, respectable, sensuous, destined to travel widely.
Scorpio:	Querulous, proud, lacking in wealth.
Sagittarius:	Powerful, rich, respectable, happy, high position.
Capricorn:	Weak, learned, immoral, unhappy, poor.
Aquarius:	Popular, respectable, timid, helpful.
Pisces:	Wealthy, learned, charitable, liked by all.

Saturn

The favourable signs for Saturn are: Taurus, Gemini Virgo, Libra, Capricorn and Aquarius.

Zodiac Sign: Influence of Saturn

Aries: Foolish, deceitful, poor, wanderer, quarrelsome.

Taurus: Successful, lustful, clever, lacking in wealth.

Gemini: Unhappy, poor, lazy, wanderer, ingenious.

Cancer: Stubborn, sick, cunning, poor.

Leo: Mean, unhappy, angry temperament, writer.

Virgo: Weak constitution, poor, immoral, quarrelsome.

Libra: Tall, tactful, famous, wealthy, respectable, lustful.

Scorpio: Fickle, arrogant, unhappy, weak health.

Sagittarius: Learned, wealthy, famous, happy during the last part of his life.

Capricorn: Wealthy, intelligent, peevish, selfish, good status.

Aquarius: Diplomatic, happy, practical, intelligent, wealthy.

Pisces: Rich, polite, happy, clever, helping nature.

Uranus

Uranus was identified as a planet in 1781 by William Herschel. It has completed only two revolutions round the Sun since its discovery. Uranus exerts its greatest influence on the sign Aquarius and therefore, this sign may be termed as its house.

Zodiac Sign: Influence of Uranus

Aries: Tall, lean and strong constitution, quick to anger, ambitious.

Taurus: Short, thickset person, passionate, revengeful, conceited.

Gemini: Tall, thin stature, generous, good-natured.

Cancer: Short corpulent person, violent, conceited, eccentric.

Leo: Tall stature, strong shoulders, proud, generous disposition.

Virgo: Short stature, lean body, studious, mean.

Libra: Tall stature, strong body, ambitious, quick temper.

Scorpio: Short and thickset body, deceitful, cunning.

Sagittarius: Tall stature, generous and independent disposition.

Capricorn: Medium height, proud, conceited.

Aquarius: Medium height, ingenious, pleasant disposition.

Pisces: Medium height, sickly, dejected and dull.

Neptune and Pluto: Neptune was discovered in 1846 and Pluto in 1930. Their movement is extremely slow. Hence it will be many years before reliable information as to the kind of persons produced by them in the various signs can be ascertained. Neptune exerts its greatest influence on the sign Pisces, and Pluto on the sign Scorpio. They may, therefore, be termed as their 'houses'.

As generally understood, the disposition, effected by Neptune is that of an institutional, impulsive, restless, doubtful, ambitious and sensual person, inclined towards spiritualism and occultism. Pluto indicates an impulsive, stubborn and violent nature.

Rahu and Ketu: There is much difference of opinion about the favourable signs of the two nodes – Rahu and Ketu. They are considered benefic when they are in the signs owned by benefic planets or are in the company of benefic planets. They are considered harmful when they are in the signs owned by malefic planets or are in the company of malefic planets. When alone, they act like Saturn and Mars, respectively.

Planetary Effects on Houses

Each house of a horoscope indicates or signifies several matters which have already been explained. A house is also represented by one or more planets which are called significators or *Karakas* of that house. The significators of different houses have been given.

When the lords of several houses and their respective significators are related to each other either through conjunction or aspect, they bestow positive effects on the native concerned.

Some planets, however, do not yield good results if posited in the houses of which they are the significators. Mars in the 3rd, Mercury in the 4th, Jupiter in the 5th and Venus in the 7th do not produce good results. However, Jupiter in the 2nd and Saturn in the 8th House increase wealth and longevity, respectively.

Planetary Effects on the Houses

The effects that the nine planets, as well as Rahu and Ketu have on the twelve houses are given below:

The Sun:

1st House: Healthy, proud, prosperous, daring, obstinate, lazy.

2nd House: Good income but loss of money, stubborn, a facial disease, stammering.

3rd House: Bold, prosperous, famous, hot-tempered.

4th House: Intelligent, reputed but devoid of happiness, comforts and house.

5th House: Poor, intelligent, unhappy, few children.

6th House: Bold, successful, wealthy, tactful.

7th House: Some trouble in married life, humiliated by women, impatient, irreligious.

8th House: Eye troubles, few issues, loss of money, ill-health, sudden gains.

9th House: Wealth, children and happiness, friction with father, lucky, successful.

10th House: Endowed with status, fame, power, health and children.

11th House: Learned, wealthy, long life, success, status.

12th House: Defective eyes, poor, base, no happiness from children.

The Moon:

1st House: Modest, fickle, romantic, easygoing, obstinate.

2nd House: Rich, soft-spoken, charming, intelligent, large family.

3rd House: Cruel, unscrupulous, miserly, sickly.

4th House: Happy, well-educated, blessed with fame and friends, owning vehicles, sensuous.

5th House: Good life, children and position.

6th House: Idler, poor, stomach complaints, many enemies, servile to the fair sex.

7th House: Passionate, zealous, fond of the opposite sex, successful.

8th House: Fickle-minded, few children, ill-health, early death of mother.

9th House: Popular, wealthy, religious, successful, good reputation and children.

10th House: Wealthy, popular, intelligent, good status, passionate.

11th House: Long life, wealthy, learned, many children and friends, good status.

12th House: Miserable, lazy, wicked, eye complaints or defect in some limb.

Mars:

1st House:	Adventurous, strong, hot-tempered, cruel, fickle, possessing marks of injuries.
2nd House:	Harsh-tongued, wicked, unpopular, devoid of learning and money.
3rd House:	Intelligent, courageous, unpopular, few brothers.
4th House:	Loss of mother, friends, happiness and comforts, quarrelsome.
5th House:	Loss of happiness and sons, cruel, unprincipled.
6th House:	Wealthy, powerful, lazy, lustful, mean, successful against enemies.
7th House:	Unhappy married life, passionate, unsuccessful.
8th House:	Poor, no marriage, short life.
9th House:	Cruel, stubborn, loss of father.
10th House:	Popular, clever, healthy, famous and powerful.
11th House:	Learned, wealthy, happy, influential.
12th House:	Defective eyesight, cruel, unsuccessful, poor.

Mercury:

1st House:	Learned, intellectual, clever, polite.
2nd House:	Wealthy, intelligent, clever, many children.
3rd House:	Clever, cruel, tactful, diplomatic.
4th House:	Intelligent, learned, happy and wealthy.
5th House:	Learned, showy, quarrelsome, many issues, respectable.
6th House:	Quarrelsome, showy, respectable, breaks in education.

7th House: Literary ability, skilful, diplomatic, successful.
8th House: Wealthy, few issues, ill health, longevity.
9th House: Highly educated, intelligent, many children, wealthy, popular.
10th House: Rich, happy, intelligent, charitable.
11th House: Wealthy, happy, successful in business, long life.
12th House: Intelligent, worried, lustful, spendthrift, few children.

Jupiter:

1st House: Learned, highly educated, blessed with children and long life, influential leader.
2nd House: Blessed with a good partner, prosperity, learning and eloquence.
3rd House: Unscrupulous, miserly, many brothers, famous.
4th House: Well-educated, wealthy, happy, several modes of conveyance.
5th House: Intelligent, good status.
6th House: Intelligent, devoid of enemies, unlucky.
7th House: Educated, good partner, sons, diplomatic.
8th House: Long life, poor, learned, unhappy.
9th House: Famous, high position, devout and philosophical, many children.
10th House: Renowned, wealthy, ambitious, virtuous.
11th House: Very wealthy, long life, influential, philanthropic.
12th House: Unlucky, sinful, wicked, devoid of children, money and happiness.

Venus:

1st House:	Attractive personality, fortunate, bold, happy, amorous, successful, practical, long life.
2nd House:	Attractive face, happy, wealthy, educated, literary skill, sweet speech, large family.
3rd House:	Affluent, miserly.
4th House:	Happy, educated, blessed with children and affectionate mother, popular.
5th House:	Prosperous, intelligent, good status, many daughters, educated.
6th House:	Poor, sickly, issueless, no enemies, licentious.
7th House:	Querulous, lustful, unhappy married life.
8th House:	Famous, sickly, unexpected gains.
9th House:	Fortunate, endowed with sons and friends, religious, comfortable life.
10th House:	Famous, good status, popular.
11th House:	Rich, intelligent, influential, popular.
12th House:	Wealthy, miserly, sexually active, weak eyesight.

Saturn:

1st House:	Dirty, lazy, unscrupulous, cunning, sickly.
2nd House:	Diseased face, break in education, little wealth, weak eyesight, harsh-tongued.
3rd House:	Intelligent, bold, generous, wicked.
4th House:	Unhappy, devoid of mother, house and vehicle, interrupted education.
5th House:	Loss of wealth, happiness and children, wicked.
6th House:	Stubborn, clever, deaf, few children.

7th House: Mean, fickle, diplomatic, unhappy married life.
8th House: Poor, fickle, clever, few children.
9th House: Devoid of wealth, father and children, wicked, diplomatic.
10th House: Wealthy, famous, happy, intelligent, sudden rise and fall in position.
11th House: Long life, affluent, influential, learned, interrupted education.
12th House: Unpopular, poor, unhappy, many enemies, extravagant.

Uranus:

1st House: Stubborn, conceited, proud, impulsive.
2nd House: Sudden gains and sudden losses.
3rd House: Skills of creative thinking, writing and inventions, strained relations with brothers and sisters.
4th House: Estranged from parents, trouble with money or property.
5th House: Bad influence on children, love affairs.
6th House: Ill-health and troubles from enemies.
7th House: Unhappy marriage, illicit relationships with women, ill-suited for business or partnership.
8th House: Wife/husband poor, fatal accident.
9th House: Fond of occult sciences, astrology, arts and sciences, sudden foreign travel.
10th House: Leadership qualities – both creditable and discreditable, dispute with superiors.
11th House: Undependable friends.
12th House: Many secret enemies.

Neptune:

1st House: Short temper, imaginative and dreamy, inclined towards spiritualism.

2nd House: Easy money, fear of poverty.

3rd House: Courageous.

4th House: Loss of property, wealth or happiness.

5th House: Disappointment in love and from children, fondness for pleasure.

6th House: Ill-health, many enemies.

7th House: Dramatic and artistic ability, illicit relationships with the opposite sex, unfortunate marriage.

8th House: Interest in spiritualism, fatal accident.

9th House: Unethical, success in publishing and travelling, inclination towards occult studies.

10th House: Unprincipled, job-hopper, worries.

11th House: Annoyance from friends.

12th House: Fear of enemies.

Rahu:

1st House: Affable at times, cruel at other times, irreligious, sickly.

2nd House: Diseased face, peevish, hostile, stammering.

3rd House: Wealthy, courageous, powerful.

4th House: Hostile, source of annoyance to others.

5th House: Issueless, poor, stomach complaints, kind, timid.

6th House: Long life, affluent, happy, no enemies.

7th House: Sickly, arrogant, poor, adulterous.

8th House: Short life, lazy, sickly, quarrelsome.

9th House: Renowned, irreligious, leader.
10th House: Intelligent, arrogant, famous.
11th House: Wealthy, long life, learned, ear disease.
12th House: Extravagant, impolite.

Ketu:

1st House: Sickly, miserly, unhappy.
2nd House: Devoid of learning and wealthy, harsh speech.
3rd House: Wealthy, famous, adventurous, moral.
4th House: Quarrelsome, devoid of happiness and comforts, finds faults in others.
5th House: Sickly, stupid, loss of children.
6th House: Learned, famous, generous, popular.
7th House: Stupid, lazy, wanderer, may prove dangerous for life partner who is a shrew.
8th House: Miserly, sickly, licentious.
9th House: Angry, irreligious, indolent, arrogant, friction with father.
10th House: Learned, happy, religious, popular.
11th House: Respectable, wealthy, intelligent, moralist.
12th House: Shameless, committing sins secretly.